ISTIMĀ'

The Sound Way & Listening for God

Dr. Ali Hussain

Forewords by
LuFuki Ismaeel Dhul-Qarnayn
& Matt Glaser

Postscript by
Pot Amir

Cover Design:
Ashraf Bakar
Copyright © 2025 Ali Hussain
All rights reserved.
ISBN: 9781737306160

Copyright 2025 Adhwaq Publishing.
All rights reserved. No part of this book may be reproduced, stored in a retrieval system, or transmitted in any form, or by any means, electronic, mechanical, photocopying, or otherwise, without the written permission of Adhwaq Publishing.

First Edition January 2025
ISBN: 978-1-7373061-6-0
Printed in the United States of America.

Library of Congress Cataloging-in-Publication Data

TBD

Published and distributed by:
Adhwaq Publishing
Email: publishing@adhwaqcenter.org
Web: https://www.adhwaqcenter.org

Contents

Foreword by LuFuki Ismaeel Dhul-Qarnayn	xiii
Foreword by Matt Glaser	xvii
Dedication	xxi
Acknowledgment	xxiii
Preface	xxix
Introduction	31
History	43
Metaphysics	81
A Primer on *Maqāmāt*	107
Reflections	121
Conclusion	223
Postscript by Pot Amir	235

Foreword by LuFuki Ismaeel Dhul-Qarnayn

*All praise is for Allah who has blessed me with **Ismaeel** and Isaac in my old age. My Lord is indeed the **Hearer** of all prayers.*
(Ibrahim, 39)

*He is Allah: **the Creator, the Inventor, the Shaper.** He, alone, has the Most Beautiful Names. Whatever is in the heavens and the earth constantly glorifies Him. And He is the Almighty, All-Wise.*
(Hashr, 24)

*O believers! Obey Allah and His Messenger and do not turn away from him while you hear his call **(tasma'ūn)**. Do not be like those who say, "We hear," **(samī'nā)** but in fact they are not listening **(lā yasma'ūn)**. Indeed, the worst of all beings in the sight of Allah are the willfully deaf and dumb, who do not understand.*
(Anfal, 20-22)

*Those who turned a blind eye to My Reminder and could not stand **listening** to it.*
(Kahf, 101)

Art doesn't need an explanation. It's enough that it evokes the necessary emotion in the observer, for that is its goal. More often than not, context is needed to explain its history and enhance the experience further. Music, as an art form, is no exception.

The discussion of "music" is becoming more of a matter for debate due to its ubiquitous nature and its place in our everyday lives; the discussion cannot be avoided. There are more discussions on the topic among scholars and lovers of music in the Islamic context, which increases yearly. Yet, there hasn't been enough scholarly work to tip the scale on its usefulness, or rather its permissibility in Islam. Or perhaps that isn't the purpose; the continuity of this mystery and its journey is the reward itself.

For the past several years in the Detroit area, Dr. Ali Hussain, myself, many of our musicians and artists friends and family (painters, poets, writers etc.), intellectuals, and professors have had lengthy discussions of how to convey, share, and translate our experiences and study on the nature of music and the importance of utilizing the arts as a spiritual practice, to everyone who would listen from small spiritual gatherings, like Sufi meditation sessions, to universities, cafes, various art institutions, and book stores.

Often, these discussions were either before and/or after musical sessions (*samā'*), which offered each session a special personal, explorative, and participatory experience likening to ecstasy. So, it's no small wonder, especially to those who know him, that Dr. Ali Hussain would be inspired enough to produce such delicate and detailed works related to the mystery, metaphysics, and nature of sound.

His past work on the dedication of Ibn Arabi's viewpoints on music remains unparalleled when discussing the metaphysics of sound because of his ability to unearth subjects from Ibn Arabi that haven't previously been concentrated on or debated. Indeed, we are blessed to have some of those "discoveries" truncated in this book.

Between your hands is his new work of art, *ISTIMĀ': The Sound Way & Listening for God*, which offers a fresh symphonic discussion and intensity in matters of new terminologies[1], interpretations, insights, outlooks, and new meanings concerning the utilization(s)[2] of "music" in the modern age. All of these could provide the reader with new meanings and discoveries that may have been dormant.

I can assure you that is one of the intentions of this book, which is a great contribution to the discussion on the metaphysics of sound that should be held in its proper place, next to the other great modern discussions and collections in this genre, such as Hazrat Inayat Khan's *Mysticism of Sound and Music* and Victor Wooten's *The Music Lesson: A Spiritual Search for Growth Through Music*, to name a few.

---

[1] Dr. Ali Hussain's preference in using *Istimā'* instead of *Samā'* is justified from the hadith from Abu Talib al-Makki's *Qut al-Qulub*, when the Prophet ﷺ was waiting for Ayesha, may God be pleased with her, because she was late and she said, "I was listening (*astami'u*) to a recitation that I never heard the likes of its beauty." Then the Prophet (saw) went to listen to the recitation for a long period.

[2] Just like how the terminologies, interpretations, insights, outlooks, and the utilization(s) of music were dynamic differed between the first two prophetic generations compared to the third and fourth. Or between the Sufis and the philosophers.

Dr. Ali Hussain, the mystic, the scholar, the teacher, the poet, the oudist, the author, and I am happy to say, my friend and colleague, has done a massive favor for the artistic spiritual aspirant as he has reduced and saved us from many years of toil to discover and unearth this beneficial knowledge that is needed for the generations to come, and has offered in such an accessible form. And I look forward to discussing this book in universities, art institutions, study halls, and my favorite places…cafes.

Respectfully,
LuFuki Ismaeel Dhul-Qarnayn
Composer | Educator | Cultural Curator | Community Organizer

Foreword by Matt Glaser

I have just finished reading *ISTIMĀ': The Sound Way & Listening for God*, the latest indispensable offering from the wonderful and unique Dr Ali Hussain. This beautiful, moving, brave and inspiring book elicited the following reflections. The Quran tells us: "And there is not a thing, but with Us are the stores thereof And we send it not down save in appointed measure" (15:21).

One could put the meaning of this passage into colloquial English as "We have infinite treasuries of all things, but We send it down in due measure". The 'all things' of which 'the infinite treasuries of' are with the Source of all Being must include melodies, rhythms, songs, compositions, improvisations as well as all other artistic works and bits thereof!

This leads us to the vast topic of what musicians at all times and places have said about their perception of where the music they play and compose – or receive? discover? – comes from. I would like to share one such passage here, from a letter by Wolfgang Amadeus Mozart:

> When I feel well and in a good humor, or when I am taking a drive or walking after a good meal, or in the night when I cannot sleep, thoughts crowd into my mind as easily as you could wish. Whence and how do they come? I do not know, and I have nothing to do with it. Those which please me, I keep in my head and hum them; at least others have told me that I do so.
>
> Once I have my theme, another melody comes, linking itself to the first one, in accordance with the needs of the composition as a whole: the counterpoint, the part of each instrument, and all these melodic fragments at last produce the entire work. Then my soul is on fire with inspiration, if however, nothing occurs to distract my attention. The work grows; I keep expanding it, conceiving it more and more clearly until I have the entire composition finished in my head though it may be long...
>
> It does not come to me successively, with its various parts worked out in detail, as they will be later on, but it is in its entirety that my imagination lets me hear it.

(This last passage has tremendous echoes of Ibn Arabi and 'unveiling'!) If you would prefer something shorter and pithier from another titan of European art music, here are the (possibly apocryphal) last words of Bach: "Don't cry for me, for I go to where music is born", or perhaps from a modern saint of music, Leonard Cohen: "If I knew where great songs came from, I would go there more often. It is most definitely a gift."

Dr Hussain casts an enormously wide net when choosing examples in his writings, and I find this tremendously inspiring; He sees the arts through the lens of "The East and the West belong to God. Whichever way you turn, there is the Face of God." (2:115)

Likewise, the book introduces the art of *maqāmāt*, or Arabic music modalities, in a simple and straightforward manner that is very attractive for Western musicians. By beginning from the scales of Western music, then introducing microtonality, the author delivers his readers, who might be unfamiliar with this artform, onto the shore of beginning to appreciate Arabic music theory more deeply.

In this, the book demonstrates the author's knowledge of Arabic music as well as his expertise in Islamic history and metaphysics. As an oud musician and mystic, the author follows in the footsteps of Inayat Khan, Yusuf Abdul Lateef, John Coltrane and others. More importantly, he explores the spirituality of sound and music through an entirely new medium: Arabic music and Quran recitation.

Dr Hussain is a rare amalgam of scholar, mystic, historian, musician, teacher, and boy does the world need more of him! I hope that this book will have the intended revivifying effect in the Islamic world, and beyond that, I hope it reaches all people of a spiritual and artistic bent everywhere. "Verily God is beautiful, and He loves beauty."

Matt Glaser
Artistic Director
American Roots Music Program
Berklee College of Music

Dedication

To my guide, Mawlana Shaykh Hisham Kabbani, who continues to guide us from the beyond. The inspiration for this book came a few days after your passing, and that is how I know it is your gift to me, to let me know that you are still guiding me.

You were a conductor of souls while physically present with us, and we shall continue to play the symphonies you taught us, to remind, and for remembrance.

Acknowledgment

I am grateful to many for this milestone. As always, despite my shortcomings, God continues to bestow his bounty upon me in breath and sound. The Prophet Muhammad ﷺ, *al-insān al-kāmil al-tāmm* (the perfect and complete human), is not only God's best work of art, but the *haqīqa al-muhammadiyya* (Muhammadan Reality) is the very fabric of creative inspiration that sustains me in my journey.

My spiritual guides, and mirrors of the Muhammadan Reality, *al-Shaykh al-Akbar* (The Greatest Master) Muhyiddin Ibn al-'Arabi, Mawlana Shaykh Hisham Kabbani and Habib Umar b. Hafidh are the proverbial sound ink behind all my words and hymns. My gratitude also goes to my parents, the first artistic inspiration, siblings and family, especially my wife Fatima and daughter Zahra who continue to support my work despite the burdens it places on them; they are the real artists, and their melodies are the sincerest artform in my life.

It would be remiss, in a book about my journey with music, not to mention my teachers in this medium. I'm deeply grateful to my oud guides Omar Abbad, Tariq al-Jundi, Ahmad al-Khatib, Simon Shaheen, Khalid Muhammad Ali, Shereef Hussein, Tarek Abdullah, Michael Ibrahim, Fadel Motaz and others like Brendan Hogan, many of whom I never met in person yet learned an incredible amount of knowledge in this eloquent language known as Arabic music.

I also acknowledge talented musician friends who have accompanied me on this journey. First and foremost, I am deeply grateful to LuFuki Ismaeel Dhul-Qarnayn, who wrote the first foreword for this book, and his partner Tazeen Ayub whose collective band *Divine Providence* is the heart of Sufi jazz in the United States and abroad. Likewise, I am so thankful to prof. Matt Glaser, not only for writing the second foreword, but also fulfilling one of my lifelong dreams by inviting me to speak, at the prestigious Berklee College of Music in Boston, to his students about art and spirituality.

I have also been blessed over the past few decades to meet countless talented musicians in the United States. Saad Omar's friendship, artistry and support continues to inspire me. Dawud Wharnsby is the guitar whisperer whose artistry made me realize true string eloquence. Raef, Alman Nusrat, Jawad "J Mecka" Fayiz, Thalib Razi and Mounira Madison are masters of their craft and am grateful to have them in my life. Rudolph Ware, Muhajir Sayer, Baraka Blue, Babar, Shaheer Khan, Ibrahim Leone, Ibrahim, Ismaeel and others are true masters of word and beat. And how can I forget Destiny

Acknowledgment

Muhammad, harpist and musical human being who embodies true reliance upon God.

I also recognize Ed Sarath and Marcus Eliot, who allowed me to share my love for *maqāmāt* at the prestigious University of Michigan School of Music. Among their company I also include Zekkereya El-Magharbel, Jenna Yahya, Renee Yaseen, Chris Pyke and the always musical Mahdi Charrara. Kamau, Malika and the rest of the Ayubbis are inspirations in flow and melody. Mason Zantow, Jared Morningstar and the rest of Shamail Ensemble are true revivers of traditional music. And how can I forget Yusuf 'Yoshi' Misdaq, the music in human form who taught me how to dress my spirituality in the silent garment of music. And Yusuf Kudaimi, your voice is already preaching from heaven, we're all catching up.

Laith Alattar was one of the first musicians who made me fall in love with the oud. Firas Zreik, Ala Yakteen, 'Abd al-Qadir Wiswall and other friends from Simon Shaheen's Arabic music retreat are masters of their craft and my mentors, as well as friends on the path. I am also fortunate to meet many talented musicians since my relocation to Nusantara in October 2024. Ismail Saber and Mohammed Salleh are true oudists with whom I played music for hours. Dr. Kamal Sabran is a sound whisperer whose work embodies the sacred role of sound I explore in this work. And Khaitama the 'playnting' saint inspires me and shows how sound can embrace color.

The always humble Ahmad Taqiuddin performs the true humility of a musical instrument. I am also grateful for the very talented Pot

Amir who agreed to write the postscript at the book's end. Likewise, Beni Amin, Naeem al-Aydarus and Aliff Irfan are incredible young musicians whose work I eagerly follow. And I hope the movement of art that is Siddhartha Phillips never stops producing. I am also so honored to recognize my group of students from the *Path of the Artist* class, the brilliant Huda, Diyana Adi, Diyana, Nazreen, Hanisah, Hidayah, Akmal, Farhan, Shaqyl, Asyraf, Hafiz, Muqri, Dasuqee, Kautsar, John and many others.

I also acknowledge artists and musicians worldwide who continue to inspire me on my journey. Karima al-Fillali's renditions of Sufi poetry is hauntingly beautiful. Raad Nile receives through his voice and the guitar what he does not yet know. Ariff Imran shows that spirituality in Metal is possible. Amr Shalaby and Shams the Poet are true artistry and tradition in a modern garb. Constantine Weir's voice truly arrives from the beyond.

Amira Kotb and others who are still passionate about *maqāmāt* keep this artform alive. I have also been most fortunate to meet incredible musicians Nathalie Amazan and Alexandr Meriweather during one of my retreats. Yousif Abbas is not only an oud whisperer, but a mystic saint of his craft. His ability to sprint and stroll across the soundscape attests to this. Meanwhile, the way in which Dominic Flynn makes the guitar speak never ceases to dumbfound me. Giovanni Herran is a masterful wordsmith, Kareem Soussan is a bright young filmmaker and Abdullatif Kanafani is beauty in a masterful form of scent and color.

Acknowledgment

I must mention artists in other mediums whose love and company sustain me in more ways than one. Ayman Azlan the intellectual artist and Ibrahim Amjad the cinematographer have accompanied my workshops since the beginning, despite being accomplished masters of their crafts. Also hailing from Brazil, like Ibrahim Amjad, is the Christic mirror and embodiment of Divine Poetry Pedro Barbosa, a bright young star with an ancient soul. I sang *Hello Goodbye* driving with Jared Saltiel during high school; I am happy to see him an accomplished musician now. Meeting the impeccable actor and saintly spirit Ryan Potter in 2022 was medicine at a low moment in my life, and he continues to be such a healing comrade on the path.

Over the past few years, Shehryar Hussain has not only become one of my closest friends but is also poetry in motion and a brilliant filmmaker. I am honored to also witness Sherif Ibrahim's artistry of film in person, while Hana Horack and Fozia Khan are color whisperers and embodiments of the Divine Dye. Omar Syed is an inspirational interior decorator and artist who speaks through color, while Sami Ahmad and Yusuf Ansari are brilliant musicians and scientists. I am also blessed to finally meet my dear friend, impeccable artist and accomplished artpeneur Peter Gould in Malaysia, since connecting virtually five years ago. Daniel Bilog is also an artist of healing and someone I am honored to call friend.

Raza Zia and Haris are brilliant architects. Hamza Ali's dancing is a bewildering site to witness. Khwarizmi and Ashraf Bakar are masters of the lens, and the latter's brilliant graphic design and cover ornament this book. Chef Mel Dean is a food whisperer; Akhimullah and Qayyum are masters of taste and exquisite culinary artists as well. Meeting my dear friend Muhib the Writer has been a breeze of mercy. For his brilliant words are a mere glimpse of his eloquent smile. And what Muhib does with words, Uthman Hanif does with melody. My love also goes to Adzim Shahabuddin and Keanu Azman, masters of the craft of television and onscreen art. Also, Azhaan the dancer speaks volumes with few letters of the body.

Lastly, special gratitude goes to all the other artists who accompany me in the Mashraba community, especially the visionary being Joshua Beneventi, whose free spirit I pray never forgets its liberation, for it guides me and countless others. Mohammad Ziyaan and Anas are two artists of the soul who are art at heart. Also, special thanks to Mohamed Nasir and SimplyIslam for their continuous support and inviting me to Singapore and Malaysia in 2023, thereby changing my life forever. Gratitude also goes to Sacredfootsteps, Khaf Magazine and Faithfully Sustainable for investing in my work. Much love to all of you!

I also acknowledge my teachers in Sufism, beginning with my advisor Alexander Knysh, Andrew Shryock, Paul Bonner (RIP), Paul Johnson, William Chittick, James Morris, Sachiko Murata, Shaykh Adeyinka Mendes and others who held my hand as I tried to dive into the depths of Ibn al-'Arabi's ocean of Islamic metaphysics. Likewise, I must mention my high school teacher and mentor Ryan Goble, who first taught the fresh immigrant in me that pop culture has a lot more to teach us than fleeting trends, for it is history told in the first person.

Preface

Nothing in existence is mute.
— Ibn al-ʿArabi, *The Meccan Openings*

This book comes two years after *A Nostalgic Remembrance: Sufism and the Breath of Creativity*; a work that I had written inwardly over a decade, yet manifested outwardly in just 1 month, whilst teaching and contemplating the intersection of Sufi metaphysics and the creative process.

And now comes this new gift from the beyond, *ISTIMĀʾ: The Sound Way & Listening* – and lessening – *for God*, a journey that focuses on a medium that has accompanied me since childhood and which has, for over a decade, become my main spiritual and creative tongue, music.

In the proceeding dance of ink on paper, I explore three main areas: *History*, *Metaphysics* and my own personal *Reflections* as a musician and educator on Islamic mysticism and its pertinence to the creative process in contemporary spirituality.

Prior to this final meditative chapter, I also include a primer on the *maqāmāt* system, or modalities of Arabic music. In this, I am indebted to the many teachers, books and resources, many of which I mentioned in the acknowledgment above. What I provide here is hardly a comprehensive exposition, but only a simplified approach for the readers unfamiliar with Arabic music.

The canvas presented here is hardly one man's effort, rather a collaboration between many talented dispositions, albeit through these feeble hands.

Introduction

*Human beings love beautiful voices
because it reminds them of the day that God spoke to them.*
— Habib 'Umar b. Hafidh

I still remember the first time I was moved by sound. I must have been 10 years old when my father took me to the weekly Friday sermon at our local mosque in Jordan. As I heard the *mu'adhdhin*'s (caller to prayer) voice echo throughout the walls of the prayer hall, I felt tears running down my face.

I recognized at the time that what moved were not necessarily the words, for I had heard them countless times before. Rather, it was the melody with which the *mu'adhdhin* ornamented them. I recognized the melody as somber, and that its effect was augmented by the reciter's transition from a more joyous melody beforehand. I had no names or terminology to describe all of this but intuitively knew that it was true.

I never recognized the centrality of music and sound in my life until much later. My journey with art meandered around many forms, as outlined in my earlier work, *A Nostalgic Remembrance*. After migrating to the United States in 1998, my passion and aim was to become a film actor. Then, much later, when I started my doctoral research, writing became my medium of choice.

It is only in 2014, when I completed the online piano course *Musiah* that I contemplated my history with music. Since childhood I had a digital piano at home and taught myself how to have basic reading skills of sheet music. At the same time, since 2004 when I started learning the art of *tajwid* (Quran recitation and memorization), I became invested in the use of *maqāmāt* (Arabic musical modalities) in decorating Divine Speech .

In 2015, I had an experience that highlighted the sacred and therapeutic power of music. While working as a graduate instructor at the University of Michigan, I introduced students to Arabic music at the beginning of every class. In one of these sessions, I chose a piece titled *'Amiriyya* by the Iraqi oudist Naseer Shamma. The composition commemorates the bombing of a shelter in a neighborhood of Baghdad with the title's namesake during the First Gulf War.

400 women and children were incinerated during the bombing by American warplanes. I was a 6-year-old child during the war and still remember vividly huddling in the bomb shelter of our own apartment when someone came and told us that shelter 25 in

'Amiriyya was destroyed. But until that moment, when I listened to Shamma's composition along with my students, I had never confronted this memory nor realized the extent of the trauma it had imprinted in my being. As I listened to the oud resurrect the war in sound more eloquent than words, my own body shut down in stillness.

I found myself wondering: "Why did I survive as a 6-year-old while others my age perished? Where might they have been now if they had lived?" I also found myself asking the spirits of the dead: "What can I do for you?" The only response I received was this: "There is nothing you can do for us now, for we are in a better place. But do for yourself by keeping our memory alive!" Music did all of this. It heals through a confrontation with suffering dressed in haunting beauty.

When the oud finally came into my life in 2017, it married my passion for music and the Quran. Despite my love for the piano, I wanted an instrument which I could carry with me wherever I went, so I bought a guitar. What I felt quickly is a sense of imprisonment between the frets. Even though I was not trying to play Arabic microtonal music, I still felt constrained by the discrete nature of sound that I was forced to produce from the instrument.

The transition to the oud felt natural, like a culmination of a journey with intersecting itineraries. But it also opened many realizations regarding my passion for Arabic music I had not realized until I began to learn the oud. The importance of this instrument transcends its techniques and mere music theory. This realization occurred alongside and through my journey with Islamic metaphysics, specifically the teachings of *al-Shaykh al-Akbar* (The Greatest Master) Ibn al-'Arabi.

In truth, it is an alignment of many proverbial stars that facilitated the journey which culminates in this book. Since my migration to the United States as a teenager in 1997, and through my spiritual rebirth and involvement with the American Muslim community – which I outlined in *A Nostalgic Remembrance*, music gradually embodied a crisis I experienced as a first-generation Muslim immigrant in America.

Alongside the *mu'adhdhin* in Jordan, my earliest memories from the Middle East are colored by a *tarab* and *saltanah*, both of which connote a sense of 'musical ecstasy' as pertains to audience and musician respectively, that seamlessly weave together the cultures of Quran recitation and secular music. The same *maqāmāt* that decorated the recordings of Quran reciters like Mustafa Ismail also enlivened the songs of Umm Kulthum and 'Abd al-Wahab.

Despite my birth in Iraq, it is my mother's native land of Egypt that increasingly shaped my cultural – read 'musical' – literacy. The so dubbed Golden Age of Arabic music in the mid 20th century remains a constant rebuttal in my imagination to, what I still consider to be, an extreme mainstream renunciation of music in American Islam. Whereas many Muslims in the West, even some of those who play or listen to music, consider it to be in contention with a believer's relationship to the Quran, 20th century Egypt proves otherwise.

In many ways, the recordings of Mustafa Ismail, music of Umm Kulthum and *taqāsīm* (improvisations) of Riyad al-Sunbati became a sonorous safe space where I could seclude myself, to recharge and recalibrate. More importantly, Ibn al-'Arabi set me on a path to reflect and situate the metaphysics of sound, as pertaining to Arabic music specifically, within my own journey in this craft.

The oud, as a fretless instrument embodies my own diaspora from Iraq after the First Gulf War and migration across boundaries and passports. It holds within its aging wood the genealogy of the guitar and lute, and rebels against a world beset by warfare and turmoil, Huntington's favorite *Clash of Civilizations*, as it welcomes both eastern and western music in its embrace.

My relationship with the oud specifically and Arabic music generally grew stronger as I also began to teach online and on-site workshops on the intersection of Islamic spirituality and creativity. Since founding my nonprofit organization, the *Adhwaq Center for Spirituality, Culture and the Arts* in its earliest stages in 2018, I have taught many courses on the sacredness of the craft and arts that delivers me to the material presented in this book.

I am also deeply grateful that this book will be the first major milestone since my relocation to Malaysia in October 2024. I am deeply grateful to my friends Dr. Sohaib Mohiuddin, Osama Syed and others at *Green Medical Network Group* (GMNG) for their support. My position as senior creative advisor at this incubator, since 2021, matures with my current additional role as president of the *Art of Healing* (AOH) project, where I explore our objective to 'curate spaces for artists to cultivate their creativity at the intersection of science, faith and culture' among Malaysian Muslim artists. I am also deeply grateful to Salman Riaz, our lead sponsor, whose generosity allows this journey to unfold.

A seal of affirmation of my decade-long journey with music and spirituality came in September 2024 when I was invited to the prestigious Berklee College of Music in Boston, at the behest of dear friend and master violinist Matt Glaser to give a two-hour workshop to his students about the 'artist as a spiritual path'. I am not exaggerating when I say that the impetus and confidence to write this book reached a zenith because of that visit to Berklee.

My reflections on the sacredness of the craft were shaped by conversations with fellow teacher Adeyinka Mendes and my spiritual guide Shaykh Hisham Kabbani. The former enlightened me on the centrality of craft as a path to *walāya* (sainthood) in traditional African societies, contrary to the contemporary Muslim impetus to restrict this path to religious scholarship.

Meanwhile, since accompanying Shaykh Hisham in 2015, I have become increasingly amazed by the number of artists in his circle of disciples. These are not only artists who practice their craft as a hobby. Rather, their spiritual path unfolds through the very technicality of their creative medium. With every verse of poetry, brushstroke of paint or pluck of a string they receive gnosis from God through their craft.

All of this clarified and rendered vivid what I had become certain of through my study of Ibn al-'Arabi and Islamic history, that the importance of music specifically and art generally for a community of faith is not mere entertainment but rather is, for the masses, the medium of choice for spiritual expression and their door to *walāya* (sainthood) and the summit of mastery.

But music, above all other art forms, seems to have an almost primordial power. The Indian Sufi mystic Hazrat Inayat Khan explained it best in *Mysticism of Sound and Music*: whatever colors cannot express, words can, but what even words fail to capture only sound can embrace. While I acknowledge my bias as a musician, I also present this superiority of music after a journey across the landscapes of creative writing as well as being born into a family of visual artists, as mentioned in *A Nostalgic Remembrance*.

Despite my slight disagreement with Hazrat Inayat Khan, that color is more eloquent than spoken language, I am in total agreement with him regarding the superior ability of sound to capture meaning. To recapitulate what my guide Habib Umar b. Hafidh mentioned at the beginning of this chapter, that "human beings love beautiful voices because it reminds them of the day that God spoke to them", undoubtedly God picked sound as the first movement of creation for a reason.

I begin this book with this last sentence through three different meandering approaches: history, metaphysics and personal reflections. Unlike *A Nostalgic Remembrance*, which contained approximately 8 chapters, I have opted here to include only three, with a more focused attention on sound and music. These tripartite themes also summarize my own journey with this medium throughout my life.

In *history*, I explore the prevalence of sound and music in Islamic history, beginning with that primordial utterance *kun* (Be!) with which God created everything other than Himself. I then look at the importance of this in the life of the Prophet Muhammad ﷺ and the nascent Muslim community. Thenceforth, I take various stops throughout history to highlight the important contributions of Muslims to the development of music and musical theory.

My aim in this chapter is to problematize the mainstream misconception among many Muslims today that music is *harām* (forbidden). I hope to show that not only did Muslims in the past play music and make musical instruments but more importantly contributed immensely to the craft's theory and practice, even influencing much of the world's music today.

In the second chapter, *Metaphysics*, I stop at one momentous milestone in Islamic history with *al-Shaykh al-Akbar* (The Greatest Master) Muhyiddin Ibn al-'Arabi and his metaphysics of sound and music. Much of the research presented in this section will be from my earlier paper, "Divine Audition in an Akbarian Court" with added excerpts from Ibn al-'Arabi's two key works, *The Meccan Openings* and *Bezels of Wisdom*. I also include here wisdoms from other Sufi mystics, including my two guides Habib Umar b. Hafidh and Shaykh Hisham Kabbani.

The largest chapter will be the last, *Reflections*, where I excavate from the first two sections and my own journey with sound, music and the oud various lessons on life and 'what it means to be human' to share with you, the reader. It is here that I hope to highlight how music, and by extension all arts, are not just mere crafts but more importantly principles and movements in life. Every note, melody, modulation, crescendo and glissando translates into human action; I pray we can decipher this together.

In writing this book, I am inspired by many works alongside all the teachers, friends and guides I have already mentioned. Hazrat Inayat Khan's *Mysticism of Sound and Music* remains the standard, I believe, in exploring the wisdom of life through this artform. As my friend and jazz musician LuFuki emphasizes, one would be hard-pressed to find a famous jazz musician in America, from Yusuf Abdul Latif to Miles Davis, without a copy of Khan's masterpiece somewhere in their library.

A second book comes from a student in Khan's Sufi order, the Inayatiyya. W.A. Mathieu's *A Musical Life* is a deep meditation on life in music and the music in life. The author's unique ability to think of his craft through the dual lenses of microcosm/macrocosm makes this work a must-read for anyone interested in music as a sacred movement. Also, the conversational style of this work inspires my own confidence to regard my readers during this journey as companions on the path, as opposed to an audience at a lecture hall.

The third work is Victor Wooten's *The Music Lesson: A Spiritual Search for Growth Through Music*, which stands as the most liberating exposition on music in daily life and necessary this is for mastering one's craft. In other words, one needs to become music to be a musician. Also, the author's own status as a prodigy bassist reveals a nuanced journey with ups and downs that gifts confidence to those struggling on their trek to the summit.

I came across Rick Rubin's *A Creative Act* soon after publishing *A Nostalgic Remembrance* and was astonished to find entire paragraphs in both our books mirroring each other in harmony. I received this serendipity as an affirmation of my own reflective journey on art and the creative process, given Rubin's expertise as a producer in the music industry for 19 years. What I bring from him into this book is an urgency to render the meandering complexity of Ibn al-'Arabi's metaphysics in a simple language.

Other important works include Johnny Faraj and Sami Abu Shumays' *Inside Arabic Music* and Kristina Nelson's *The Art of Reciting the Quran*, both of which should be considered central references on *maqāmāt* in secular Arabic music and Quran recitation respectively. Alongside these sources, countless others on art the creative process have shaped my vision and approach in this book.

Indeed, as poet Charles Bukowski states: "The intellectual makes what is simple difficult while the artist makes what is difficult simple." For this reason, and others that I have outlined in *A Nostalgic Remembrance*, I opt once again to omit extensive footnotes and cited references in this work. Most of the sources mentioned will be in the first two chapters, but only minimally to help the reader pursue further research on their own if they are so interested.

This work, like its predecessor, is not intended to be an academic contribution, but rather a pertinent meditation for the masses. In that regard, the only reason I am including the first two chapters on history and metaphysics is to share with readers the palette with which I weave my own reflections on this passion and the craft of music. I am deeply convinced that it would be a disservice to this sacred medium to pursue this project otherwise.

I conclude with one final point regarding the title of the book. What is ISTIMĀ'? I contemplated using the commonly used derivative SAMĀ', which translates to 'auditory session of listening to music or sacred chants'. However, due to the overuse of the latter term in books and other forms of media, I decided to introduce this more intensive – albeit rarely used – related term. It is also the word commonly used in the Quran as a command to 'listen attentively', all of which harmonizes well with the journey towards sound and music that we wish to undertake in this book.

History

They are not from us, those who do not melodiously recite the Quran
– Prophet Muhammad ﷺ

Islam began, like creation, with sound. Just as the Divine Creative Command *Kun!* (Be) reverberated with life and spirit throughout the canvas of creation, so did *Iqra'* (Recite) also reverberate in the being of the Prophet Muhammad ﷺ during his seclusion in the cave of Hira atop Jabal al-Nur (Mountain of Light) that overlooked Mecca. And just as sound came before form in the movement of cosmic creativity, so did the voice of the Holy Spirit, Archangel Gabriel also precede the appearance of his form in front of the Prophet ﷺ atop the mountain.

Then there was silence for what seemed like an eternity, as the Prophet ﷺ tried to recuperate from this sonorous experience by asking his family to cover him and he shivered with 'sound divine energy'. When the revelation resumed its descent, some six months later, the Prophet ﷺ described its arrival also as soundscape. Sometimes it arrived like the 'ringing of a bell, humming of bees or a metal chain dragged across rocks'. A primordial sound, signaling the arrival of the angelic messenger, unfolded into the sound of Divine Speech in the heart of the human messenger.

The Quran continued to be transmitted orally from the Prophet ﷺ to his family and companions. It was only written after his transition to the Divine Abode at the behest of his companion and *khalifa* (leader of the Muslims after him) Abu Bakr, due to the death of Quran memorizers among the prophetic companions. This oral transmission was stamped with sacred musicality as evident in the *hadith* (statement) of the Prophet ﷺ, mentioned at the beginning of this chapter: "They are not from us, those who do not melodiously recite the Quran."

But this is not the only evidence. The Prophet ﷺ also said: "Beautify the Quran with your voices" and more poignantly "God listens more attentively to the reciter with a beautiful voice than one of you listens to their musical instrument." Lest the last *hadith* be taken as a disparagement of musical instruments, note that the Prophet ﷺ also praised those among his companions who recited the Quran beautifully by comparing their voices to a "reed flute from among those given to the people of David."

Sound also played a most intimate role during the Prophet's miraculous *mi'raj* (ascension) journey to the Divine Presence. Prior to entering the Divine Court, above the seven heavens, the Prophet

⌘ entered a place, beyond space and time, which Ibn al-'Arabi describes as being of extreme *wahsha* (loneliness). Suddenly, he heard the voice of Abu Bakr and felt tranquil. When he asked God about this incident, he received the response: "Because you were lonely, I created an angel with the form and voice of Abu Bakr to keep you company." And yet, the Prophet ⌘ did not see the angel, only heard its voice. Sound was enough to alleviate *wahsha*.

There seems to be a misconception among many Muslims today that music contends with the Quran, disregarding the fact that Divine Revelation already came married to musicality. As a matter of fact, the Quran can become the very wellspring of inspiration for musicians, as evident in the 'Golden Age of Arabic Music' which we will discuss towards the end of this chapter. But already during the life of the Prophet ⌘, he had married musicality to the Quran by using the term *taghanni*, a derivative of *ghinā'* (singing) to refer to melody.

However, it was not just music, but all the arts had thrived during the life of the Prophet ⌘ who even built in his mosque a podium for the poet Hassan b. Thabit. The Messenger ⌘ also used abstract art to convey revelation and allowed drumming, singing and dancing in the mosque and his private home as well. And this continued after his transition to the Divine Abode.

When Hassan stood on his podium to recite poetry, after the Prophet's passing, the ruler at the time 'Umar b. al-Khattab ordered him to stop. Hassan's blunt response was: "Someone much better than you liked what I am doing." But it was sound and melody that made the inhabitants of Medina believe that the Prophet ﷺ had returned to physical life. When the Prophet's *mu'adhdhin*, Bilal migrated to Damascus after the former's transition, he was visited by the Prophet ﷺ in a dream: "What is this cold-heartedness Bilal, haven't you missed us?"

When Bilal returned to visit Medina, the grandsons of the Prophet ﷺ, Hasan and Husayn, still children at the time, asked him to call the *adhān* (call to prayer) as he did for their grandfather. After much hesitation, Bilal filled the corners of Medina with his voice as he used to do during the Prophet's lifetime, and all the people came out of their homes believing the Prophet had returned. When Bilal reached the phrase: "I bear witness that Muhammad is the Messenger of God" he wept profusely, as did all of Medina. The narrator of this story states that the prophetic city never wept as much after the Prophet's passing as they did that day when Bilal returned and called the *adhān*.

Yes, Islam was born and thrived through sound, and melody was the means through which the prophetic presence was felt and resurrected. In other words, sound and melody are a séance in Islam, at least for that early generation. This is also beautifully embodied in a conversation between a companion and Anas b. Malik, one of the closest companions of the Prophet ﷺ. When the latter states: "I have not smelled musk sweeter than the fragrance of the Prophet ﷺ nor touched silk softer than his hands", the former asks: "You can almost see the Prophet now and hear his melody, can you not?" to which Anas replied: "Yes, by God, I can."

For that early Muslim generation, the five senses were in communication. Igniting the spark of the faculties of smell and touch was a shaman dance that awakened vision and sound. And the goal was the Prophetic voice that recited Divine Speech as intended by God and that continues to reverberate from the beyond. As he ﷺ himself said: "My life is good for you and my passing is better for you, since your deeds are shown to me. Whatever good I find I praise God and whatever bad I find I ask Him to forgive you."

But the larger context of Mecca and Medina is also important in this regard. Both cities, as well as the larger Arabian Peninsula hosted a very musical and orally oriented society. Pre-Islamic Arabs launched wars and negotiated peace through poetry. The rich non-Arabs who brought their caravans during the Hajj season and who thought that Arabs were 'vagabonds of the desert' with nothing to contribute to society save being custodians of God's house built by Abraham, were humbled to learn about the hundreds of Arabic words to describe a lion, mountain or river.

The Arabs' mastery of speech was almost miraculous. They could improvise poetry that is recited from left to right as *madīh* (praise) but also from right to left as *hijā'* (irreverence); this is how countless poets escaped captivity from rival tribes. Most amazingly, poets were able to rectify the meter of their verses by reciting them into barrels of water and counting the ripples that their words made. To such a people who had mastered language came a miracle in the form of revelation, speech and melody.

Indeed, Muslims today should be more aware of the power of sound, melody and music than people of other faiths, but let us follow the trajectory of history to see where the fracture occurs. For many generations and centuries, the people of Medina were known as *ahl al-ghinā'* (people of singing). Even during the Prophet's lifetime, as the historian Qurtubi shows, there were female companions who had stage names, such as Jamila, the private singer of the Prophet's wife A'isha, and Arnab the 'singer of Medina'.

But it wasn't just voice-singing. The nephew of the Prophet's cousin and son-in-law Ali b. Abi Talib, Abdullah b. Ja'far, was himself an oudist who used to host sessions of *samā'* in his house with singers. During one such event, a wedding where another companion was present, a third walked into the house and proclaimed: "How shameful that this should occur in the house of the Prophet's companions", to which both Abdullah and the second companion replied: "We have permission from the Prophet to express joy during weddings. If you wish, you can stay or leave!"

In his groundbreaking work, *The Great Book on Music*, the Muslim philosopher al-Farabi highlights the prevalence of a music culture in Medina, where one well-known musician/dancer wore bells all over his body and had the ability to produce any melody by moving the right limbs in a particular motion. Al-Farabi's work itself is a testimony to the importance of music in Muslim culture at the time.

Still considered to be one of the authoritative texts in the genre, this thousand-page tome was one of the earliest expositions on *maqāmāt* (Arabic musical modalities) and laid the foundations for concepts central to Western music such as the circle of fifths.

Remarkably, al-Farabi associates *maqāmāt* with specific times of the day as remedies for physical illnesses. For instance, if you play or listen to *maqām nihāwand* on the night of Wednesday, it will cure all physical ailments. Prior to al-Farabi, the 'first teacher' al-Kindi regarded music even more seriously. He held that a musician who intentionally plays a somber melody for a sick person to be *āthim* (sinful), while playing a happy melody for the same individual would be considered a *hasana* (good deed), since he believed that music can either kill or heal a human being.

This is much different than the contemporary Muslim approach to music which regards it as either forbidden or, if permissible, as frivolous entertainment. Early philosophers like al-Kindi and al-Farabi considered music to be a sacred trust and responsibility. They perceived it as energy that can be used for good, in which case it would be an act of worship, or evil, in which case it is as grievous as murder in the hands of one who does not know how to wield it.

The reputation of the people of Medina as *ahl al-ghinā*[3] continued for centuries. As al-Qurtubi mentions, various scholars of *hadith*

---

[3] Many of the sources mentioned here can be found in "Imam Malik Learned Singing as a Young Man. A *Hadith* Scholar Plays Music for His

from the prophetic city migrated to Baghdad, whence scholars and students alike sought to learn from them. In two unique incidents, one of the scholars of Baghdad heard loud singing from the house of the visiting Medinan scholar, Ibrahim b. Sa'd al-Zuhri. He was shocked to find the renowned scholar of *hadith* singing. He scolded him and swore to never receive any *hadith* transmission from him. Al-Zuhri was so upset by this behavior that he swore to never narrate *hadith* in Medina save that he would first sing beforehand.

The next day, the Abbasid caliph Harun al-Rashid called the Medinan scholar to his court, for he had heard of the confrontation between him and the other local scholar. The caliph asked the al-Zuhri about a *hadith* and the latter immediately requested: "Bring me the oud!" The caliph asked: "The oud for burning [incense] or *tarab* [musical ecstasy]?" Al-Zuhri replied: "The one for *tarab*!" The caliph smiled and asked for an oud, whence al-Zuhri played music, sang then recited *hadith*.

A similar incident involves yet another 'singing' scholar of *hadith* from Medina, al-Fayruzabadi, who relocated to Baghdad. When local scholars confronted him about his proclivity to singing and how it does not befit his status as a *hadith* scholar, the latter further confused his interlocutors by stating: "I will supplicate for you especially during *samā'* [musical audition]," which caused his detractors to

---

Students and a Hanbalite Makes Mules Dance", https://www.aljazeera.net/turath/longform/2022/1/11/علماء-موسيقيون

wonder: "Does he believe that the session of *samā'* is *sā'at istijāba* [a time when prayers are answered]?"

One of the crucial moments in the history of music in Islam occurred in the 9th century, when the musician Ziryab migrated from Baghdad to Andalucia, taking the oud with him. When he arrived in the West, the Umayyad caliph Abdul Rahman II invited him to his court and asked the musician to demonstrate his abilities. Ziryab played a joyous melody for 30 seconds and made everyone, including the king, smile. Then, he played a somber melody for 30 seconds and made everyone cry. The caliph was so impressed by the musician that he sponsored a conservatory for Ziryab to teach music.

More importantly, the Christian troubadours were so impressed by the oud that they adopted the instrument and later developed it into the lute, the ancestor of the guitar. In this way, the oud, a middle eastern instrument that preceded Islam, thrived among Muslim musicians and directly influenced Western music and the invention of the guitar, a trend that continues until modernity. It is significant that a medieval Muslim caliph had sponsored the building of a music school in Andalucia.

Starting in the 10th century, there was a tremendous cultural and intellectual efflorescence across all Muslim lands. Most notably, the introduction of Neoplatonism through the Fatimid Dynasty created positive ripple effects that spanned east and west.[4] During this

---

[4] For more on this, refer to Yusuf Casewit's *The Mystics of al-Andalus*.

period, there emerged a voluminous text known as *Rasā'il Ikhwān Ahl al-Safā* (Treatise of the Brethren of Purity), of uncertain authorship. Nonetheless, the identity of its writer is less important than the content of the work itself.

This book emerges as a template for a larger genre of writings that symbolized the epitome of Islamic intellectual tradition. An encyclopedic work that covers the foundations of metaphysics, storytelling and education, the *Rasā'il* was a comprehensive discourse on reality. Among its countless chapters, the one on education is of crucial importance here. This section outlines a trivium and quadrivium of disciplines that every student should learn prior to studying divinity and metaphysics. Unsurprisingly, the first topic is musical theory as a foundational discipline in mathematics. This is followed by geometry, logic, philosophy, biology, chemistry, physics, astronomy/astrology and finally divinity or metaphysics.

The greatest contribution to the metaphysics of sound and music occurred among Sufi masters and authors. Already in al-Qushayri's celebrated 10th century treatise *al-Risala* [The Qushayrian Treatise] we find an entire section devoted to *samā'*, which has incidentally been omitted from recent editions of the original Arabic, for reasons that will soon become clear. In this section, al-Qushayri describes the ability to listen attentively to music as a unique rank exclusive to the *fuqarā'*, or those who have ascertained their absolute impoverishment and need for God.

One would be hard pressed to find a single major text of Sufism from this period, until the 17th or 18th century, without a discussion of *samā'* and musical instruments. Prior to continuing in this historical outline, I would like to highlight that the common criticism by some Muslims today that medieval *samā'* did not involve musical instruments is not really valid for two important reasons. First, *samā'* did often include musical instruments like the reed flute, oud and drums. Second, even if we were to restrict *samā'* to religious chants, already in the 9th century Muslim philosophers like al-Farabi had considered the human voice to be the greatest musical instrument.

The reviver of Islam in the 11th century, Abu Hamid al-Ghazali famously said: "Whoever is not moved by spring and its roses or the oud and its strings, then their disposition is corrupt, for which there is no cure." It is noteworthy that today al-Ghazali is considered to be the father of moral and ethical Sufism, whose magnum opus *Ihyā' 'Ulūm al-Dīn* (Reviving the Religious Sciences) is taught and translated across east and west; yet, this quote is nowhere mentioned nor elaborated upon.

Al-Ghazali also uses as proof for the permissibility of music the singing of birds and animals. And since musical instruments, especially wind instruments, are designed to mimic the vocal system of birds and animals, they cannot possibly be forbidden. It is for this reason that I often wonder what birds might think of religious extremists who think that music is not allowed? Especially since music and singing is the only communication birds have. Would God create such animals to speak in a *harām* way?

The epitome of Sufi metaphysics and writing was in the 12th-14th centuries, during which period the Muslim world hosted two giants of Islamic spirituality: Muhyiddin Ibn al-'Arabi and Jalal al-Din Rumi. In the following chapter, on *Metaphysics*, I dedicate an extensive discussion to Ibn al-'Arabi's metaphysics of sound and music. For now, let us linger for a moment with Rumi's attention to the sacred role of music in one's journey to God.

The Sufi poet begins his celebrated compendium of poetry, the *Mathnawi*, also known at the time as the 'Quran in Persian', with the verse: "Have you not listened to the reed and how it laments its separation from the reed-bed?" The rest of the hundreds of couplets are filled with contemplations on music and musical instruments, but one important remark is in order. An anecdote transmitted by some saints regarding the origins of the reed-flute highlights the sacred imagination surrounding music in Islam.

It is related that the Prophet ﷺ had whispered secret knowledge to his cousin, son-in-law and 'gate to the city of prophetic knowledge' Ali b. Abi Talib and entrusted him not to reveal it to anyone. Ali was burdened with the heaviness of the knowledge he had received and went into the desert. He found a dry well and spoke the secret into the depths, hoping that no one would hear it. After he left, the well overflowed with water and the surrounding area became a reedbed. A shepherd passing by with his cattle took one of the reeds and shaped it into a flute to guide the animals.

The sound of the music reached the ear of the Prophet ﷺ across the distance, whence he asked Ali: "Did you utter the secret?" This translation of prophetic knowledge into music is a continuation of the sacralization of art prevalent in the Quran and *hadith* literature, as we discussed previously. We also have other anecdotes from Rumi's life pertaining to music. In the first, whilst listening to music, a man reproached him: "When we listen to this, we can hear the gates of paradise closing" to which Rumi replied: "They are closing for you but opening for us."

In the second, Rumi was asked: "What type of music is forbidden?" to which he replied: "The sounds of spoons and forks heard by the poor and hungry." Such anecdotes continue throughout the centuries. In one such instance, the 18th century Sufi mystic Abd al-Ghani al-Nabulusi was reproached in his own Sufi lodge by a religious scholar who saw countless stringed instruments hanging on the walls of the lodge. Without uttering a word, al-Nabulusi pointed with his finger at the instruments, each of which began to make loud *dhikr* (remembrance of God).

Here, we are moved to highlight the centrality of sound, melody and musicality in Sufi practices, specifically breathwork and *dhikr*. Already during the generation of the Prophet ﷺ it is narrated that one knew the Prophet ﷺ and his companions had completed prayer by the loud *dhikr* they made afterwards. The Prophet ﷺ also stated in one of his teachings: "Remember God until they call you crazy!"

And since the advent of Sufi *turuq* (paths and fraternities), melody has always been married to the practice of *dhikr*.

The purpose of *nagham* (melody) in divine remembrance is the same as in Quran recitation: to remember and recollect, an attempt at approximating the experience of listening to the Prophet directly during his lifetime. Let us not forget Anas b. Malik's own recollection of the Prophet through the senses of smell and touch which helped resurrect the prophetic company in sound and vision. And alongside melody, breath also becomes the central means through which the *hadra* (divine presence) can be experienced.

Perhaps, just as the Prophet ﷺ had tethered meaning in Divine Speech to melody, in the *hadith* with which we started this chapter, so have Sufi masters also married meaning and gnosis in *dhikr* to melody. In other words, melody is not mere ornament in Quran recitation or *dhikr*, but rather a necessary key to unlock meaning. But this ritual is not only a standalone practice, but a principle which the seeker is moved to experience in all living things.

Indeed, as the Quran states: "There is naught a thing save that it glorifies His Praise, but you do not comprehend their glorification." This includes musical instruments. And this is the *karāma* (saintly miracle) which al-Nabulusi performed and tried to make the angry religious scholar understand: you despise musical instruments because you cannot understand the way they praise God. The very sound that these instruments produce is itself *dhikr*, as al-Nabulusi and Ibn al-ʿArabi before him would emphasize.

The importance of music and musical instruments continued until the advent of Wahhabism in the 19th century, which is a colonial implant in the heart of Islam to destroy the religion from within. In *Intellectual Life in the Hijaz Before Wahhabism*, Nasir Dumairieh shows that Muslim scholars taught music theory in Mecca and Medina, alongside the usual disciplines of theology, jurisprudence, *hadith* and Quran. Some even had sobriquets like 'al-Tanburi' (the tanbur player) or 'al-Kamanji' (the violinist). They taught classes on musical practice and held private concerts in these two sacred cities of Islam.

Then, suddenly, the onslaught of Wahhabism changed this rich cultural landscape of the heart of Islam. The people of Medina were no longer known as *ahl al-ghinā'* (people of singing). Rather, the religious extremist and founder of the Wahhabi movement Muhammad b. 'Abd al-Wahhab ordered all the people in the prophetic city to bring out their musical instruments, which he then burned in a large fire in the center of the city. We need to linger for a moment on the reason behind this hatred for the arts, and specifically music, in this modernist and fundamentalist movement.

We need to understand that Wahhabism is a colonial implant. Although religious extremism and critical opinions of music and musical instruments have existed throughout Islamic history, never did they have the currency nor exercised the violence that began with this movement. This much should be clear from our discussion thus far on the rich engagement with music among Muslims since the Prophet's time until this point. Despite the censure by some religious scholars, there were always Ziryabs, Zuhris, Fayruzabadis and Nabulusis who shaped their surroundings musically and culturally.

I propose that the reason behind this attack is colonial and political more than religious, despite the Wahhabis own immediate concerns. The British had conspired with the Ibn Abd al-Wahhab's clan to support their rule over the Arabian Peninsula, after ousting Sharif Hussain, a descendant of the Prophet Muhammad ﷺ and ruler of Mecca and Medina. The British intended for Wahhabism to be the catalyst for a Protestant Reformation from within Islam.

It is also hardly coincidental that this form of religious colonialism preceded its political counterpart and the annexation of Muslim land. The arts serve a crucial purpose in resistance: They are a remembrance of liberation and silent triumph against oppressors. The colonial empires sought to destroy these tools of Muslim storytelling, under the guise of religious vengeance, with the malicious aim that subsequent Muslim generations would forget their history and ancestry.

Unfortunately for this colonial project, poets like Mahmoud Darwish and singers like Umm Kulthum would continue to commemorate the past of liberation and solidify the sacred marriage between art and resistance. In a move perhaps unexpected by the colonial powers, after the fall of the Ottoman Empire and emergence of Arab Nationalism and the various Arab states, the legacy of art and music transitioned from religious to secular hands, all for the best.

A new genealogy emerged that tethered the old order to a new one. One example demonstrates this transition clearly. Uthman al-Mawsili, one of the renowned Quran reciters of the 19th – 20th century from Iraq, master of *maqāmāt* (musical modalities) and composer of various religious odes migrated to Iraq after British occupation and moved to Turkey before settling in Egypt. There he would become the teacher of Sayyid Darwish, a celebrated Egyptian musician and father of the songs of resistance against British occupation.

Darwish learned some of his most well-known songs, including *Zurūnī kul Sana Marra* (Visit Me Once a Year), from al-Mawsili. This chain of transmission continued from Darwish to his student, *mūsīqār al-ajyāl* (musician of the generations) 'Abd al-Wahab, not to be confused with the founder of the religious extremist movement. 'Abd al-Wahab is easily considered one of the major milestones in the 'Golden Age of Arabic Music' in the 20th century. He is also responsible for reforming the art of singing classical Arabic poetry, which he developed with his other teacher, the renowned Egyptian poet Ahmad Shawqy.

Alongside musicians and composers like 'Abd al-Wahab, Darwish, Riyad al-Sunbati, al-Mouji, al-Qasabji and later Baleegh Hamdi or singers like Umm Kulthum, 'Abd al-Haleem Hafidh, Farid al-Atrash and Najat al-Saghira, the art of Quran recitation continued to flourish in Egypt throughout the 20th century. Reciters like Muhammad Siddiq al-Minshawi, Muhammad Rif'at, Abu al-'Aynayn Shu'aysha', Abd al-Basit Abd al-Samad and the zenith of musical recitation, dubbed *amīr al-naghamāt* (prince of melodies), Mustafa Ismail continued the pre-modernist tradition of invigorating the art of Quran recitation with *maqāmāt* and melody.

However, what makes this period, the 'Golden Age of Arabic Music' unique is the marriage and harmony between the cultures of secular music and Quran recitation. As Mustafa Ismail himself mentions, Umm Kulthum used to consult him regularly on her songs. Although he never studied music formally, his mastery of *maqāmāt* made him not only a Quran reciter but a musical authority. But his life also reveals a deeper relationship and appreciation of music.

Ismail recounts the first time he was invited to recite Quran in Cairo, since most reciters like him begin their career in small villages before receiving an invitation to perform in the big city. When Ismail walked into the neighborhood where the venue was located, he passed by a café filled with oud musicians. He states he was anxious because he realized that he will be performing for a crowd of *sammī"a* (professional listeners), those who are familiar with Arabic music and *maqāmāt*.

Elsewhere, Ismail emphasizes the 'concert-like' nature of his *mehfil* (recitation *samā'* sessions). He states that his ability to recite well, or 'diversify the use of *maqāmāt* and his range of voice', depends entirely on the response of the crowd and their engagement with him. He even recounts one specific instance where a listener sitting in the front row dozed off during the recitation. Ismail realized that this was a professional listener, well-versed in *maqāmāt*. Thus, the reciter did an unexpected *naqla* (modulation) from one *maqām* to another whence the listener immediately woke up and screamed: "Allah!"

The depth of knowledge of Arabic music which the audience during this period had cannot be overstated. One can hear in some of Ismail's recordings many of the *sammī"a* request a repetition of a Quranic verse in a particular *maqām*. In some other recordings, they anticipate which verses or chapters of the Quran he will recite based on a modulation to a new *maqām*. But the question is: how and why did the audience acquire such knowledge?

First, it is worthwhile noting that the same *sammī"a* who attended the recitation *mahāfil* (sg. *mehfil*) of Mustafa Ismail also listened to the songs of Umm Kulthum and other giants of Arabic music at the time. Walking through the streets of Cairo, one could regularly hear either Ismail's recordings or Umm Kulthum's songs playing on the radio from homes and coffee shops. In other words, Arabic music was a universal vernacular in early 20th century Egypt. The masses already digested *maqāmāt*, often without knowing their names, which could be very easily learned.

Most importantly, both Quran reciters and musicians shared this language of *maqāmāt*. Often, the likes of 'Abd al-Wahab and Umm Kulthum even attended the *mehfil* of Mustafa Ismail and other Quran reciters. And so, any lines demarcating Quran recitation and secular music were blurry at best. Not only did musicians like Umm Kulthum seek the musical opinion of Quran reciters like Mustafa

Ismail, but musicians also contributed to the sacred soundscape of Egypt at the time.

A perfect example of this is Baleegh Hamdi, a prodigy young composer who wrote songs for Umm Kulthum, even though she was very selective in choosing composers many of whom were usually older than Baleegh. But this composer also had a piercing musical sixth sense. In the 1970s he reached out to the celebrated *mubtahil* (reciter of religious odes) Sayyid al-Naqshbandi because he wanted to compose a piece for him. Al-Naqshbandi was very hesitant at first, remarking that he cannot sing a melody composed by someone who writes songs for secular musicians.

The Egyptian president at the time, Anwar Sadat himself intervened and demanded: "Put Baleegh and al-Naqshbandi in a room and lock the door. They are not to leave until they compose a melody." Al-Naqshbandi agreed on one condition. He stated that he will go in the room with Baleegh; if he leaves with his turban off, that means he has agreed to work with the composer. Before going inside the recording studio, Baleegh told al-Naqshbandi: "I will compose a melody for you that will remain for 100 years."

It only took 5 minutes. Al-Naqshbandi walked out with his turban off and proclaimed: "Baleegh must be possessed by a jinn, his genius is impossible." And the musician's sixth sense was correct, for the melody he had composed, *Mawlay* (My Lord), became al-Naqshbandi's most well-known piece that is still played and admired today, some 40 years since they met. Aside from explicitly religious odes such as *Mawlay*, secular composers like Baleegh also contributed to the sacred soundscape in other ways.

When one analyzes the lyrics written by these composers or even those words around which they composed their songs, one finds the aura of medieval Sufi poetry still moving their pens and creative spirits. A perfect example is Umm Kulthum's song *al-Atlal* (The Ruins), which is considered by many critics to be the greatest Arabic song of the 20th century. The lyrics were written by Ibrahim Naji and the melody composed by Riyad al-Sunbati.

The opening verse: "Oh my heart, do not ask about love! For it was an imaginal altar that dissipated" might as well be from Rumi's *Mathnawi* or written by one of the other countless Sufi poets. Even later composers like Baleegh excavated this Sufi spirit in their songs. This is evident, for instance, in *Ba'sha'ak* (I adore you), written and composed by Baleegh in colloquial Egyptian. One finds this Sufi spirit in verses like: "I adore you. I am entirely for you. O you, who conquered my spirit with their love. The past is yours; tomorrow is yours and what is after also yours." This trend continues in Egyptian music until the 1990s and turn of the century.

Soon after Husni Mubarak became president of Egypt in 1980, he invested in Egyptian television and cinema. This ushered another transition in Arabic music, like the one at the turn of the 20th century at the hands of Darwish and 'Abd al-Wahab. Whereas the heart of musical production, before the 80s, was in large ensembles on the stage with singers like Umm Kulthum or 'Abd al-Halim, the *titr* (film or television soundtrack) became the new site for musical growth in Egypt towards the end of the 20th century.

This also gave rise to a new class of composers and singers, with some overlap from the past generation. Most notably, Baleegh Hamdi continued to compose and contribute to the *titr* genre, including his masterpiece *Bawwabt al-Halawani*, a historical epic on Egypt during the Ottoman period. Among the new class of composers, most important are 'Ammar al-Shiree'i, Michel al-Masri, Yasir Abd al-Rahman and others. Alongside these composers, there also emerged poets who provided the lyrics for these musicians and their *titr* (soundtrack).

Most notable among these poets, many of whom wrote in vernacular, are Sayyid Hijab and 'Abd al-Rahman al-Abnoudi. We also find new singers who brought these lyrics and melodies to life, including Ali al-Hajjar, Muhammad al-Hilw, Angham and others. Perhaps one of the most celebrated of these compositions is the soundtrack for *Layali al-Hilmiyya* (The Nights of Hilmiyya), a sociohistorical epic recounting Egypt during British occupation and the transition from monarchy to Arab nationalism.

The lyrics written by Sayyid Hijab, composed by Michel al-Masri and sung by al-Hilw highlight an important change in the spiritual landscape of Egyptian society:

> Where does anguish come from?
> From the changes of the age
> Where does desire come from?
> From the harmony in winds

> Where does darkness come from?
> From greed and stubbornness
> Where does contentment come from?
> From belief in the divine decree
> From the brokenness of the spirit, in the heart of nation
> Comes the death throes of longing in the prison of bodies
> From the fermentation of the dream, morning comes
> One returns of estranged home, no family or place
> Why, oh time, did you not leave us innocent?
> Why are you taking us to a road of no return?
> Our deepest wounds yield to mockery
> And the purist laugh is lost in a sea of tears

These words reveal an intentional phrasing and depiction of Egyptian spirituality. This is also a drastically different vision than Egypt prior to the fall of the Ottoman Empire.

Since the fall of the monarchy and rise of pan-Arab nationalism under Gamal Abdul Nassir, Egypt ceased to be one of the seats of the Islamic caliphate. Egyptians, both the government and society, became keenly aware of the diverse demographic of their country. This new national vigor demanded a spiritual outlook, universal in its language, that can accommodate both Muslims and the considerably large Coptic Christian population, who are Egypt's original inhabitants.

To this end, Nassir's regime employed many Egyptian artists, including Naguib Mahfouz whose novels *Wlad Haritna* (Children of Our Neighborhood), *Hadith al-Sabah al-Masa'* (Talk of Morning and Night), *Kifah Uhmus* (Uhmus' Struggle) and others depicted Egyptian spirituality not as purely Islamic, but rather nationalistic and, most importantly, tethered to the country's pre-Islamic heritage: ancient Egypt.

During an interview, the Sufi actor Ahmad Maher was asked about his role in the TV adaptation of Mahfouz' *Talk of Morning and Night*. A scene was shown where Maher's character sees a dream foretelling his passing. The character sells his shoe store and hires workers to dig and build his shrine. As Maher watches the character he played cry on screen, the actor's own tears flow down his face. The interviewer asks: "Why are you so emotional?" To which Maher says: "This scene shows the sanctity of death for Egyptians, since the time of the pharaohs."

What Maher is saying is that this new Egyptian spirituality regarded Sufi shrines not just as Islamic artifacts but more importantly as a continuation of an ancient Egyptian tradition: modern pyramids for the dead. It is no coincidence that in this new spiritual prism, the sanctity which modern Egyptians accord to music can be traced to the pyramids, since what we find inside these shrines are drawings of musical instruments: the oud, harp and reed flute.

This sensibility manifests in many ways. I was moved while watching a studio recording session with Abd al-Wahab in the 1990s where the conductor uttered before the first rehearsal: *Bismillah al-Rahman al-Rahim* (In the Name of God Most-Beneficent Most-Merciful), which is the beginning of almost every chapter of the Quran and considered a sacred formula initiating acts of ritual worship. But one finds that this is a common practice in Egypt, where this Quranic verse is written even on the covers of screenplays and novels.

Returning to the marriage of Quran recitation and secular music, the composer Ammar al-Shiree'i, who composed some of the greatest soundtracks during the 80's and 90's, including *Ra'fat al-Haggan*, *Hadith al-Sabah wa-l-Masa'* and others, also invited Quran reciters to his television program *Laylat al-Shiree'i* (The Night of Shiree'i). In one episode, he hosted Dr. Ahmad No'aina', a celebrated Quran reciter and student of Mustafa Ismail. The two spoke about Ismail's legacy and his ability to utilize the art of *maqāmāt* in Quran recitation.

Al-Shiree'i then did something remarkable: he gave a musical overview of Ismail's recitation, analyzing the modulations and melodic progression in select phrases and verses. The musician concluded: "If Ismail is not a musician, then we musicians have no right being in the music business." This initiative by al-Shiree'i motivated me to write my own study in Arabic, published on the website Ma3azef, titled: "The Melodic Narrative of Mustafa Ismail" where I analyzed one of his lengthy recordings (1 hour and 40 minutes) and proposed that Ismail's melodic progression is a form of *taqsīm* (improvisation).

This period also witnessed a revival of Egypt's new spiritual prism with a nationalistic tinge where many of Naguib Mahfouz' novels, with this spiritual focus in mind, were adapted into television dramas, such as *Talk of Morning and Night*. Much like the Golden Age of Arabic Music in the early to mid-20th century, the 80s and 90s also were an alignment of creative minds, such as those mentioned in the preceding paragraphs. What awaited Egyptian film, television and music in the 21st century is a much different story.

The first sign of deterioration appeared in the absence of *maqām* consciousness, not only in song and music generally but more importantly Quran recitation. However, it is worthwhile mentioning that since the late 90s until today there emerged pockets in Egypt that aim to preserve this heritage, in the form of salons where musicians perform the songs of Umm Kulthum and other giants from the Golden Age. Some of these musicians even performed in Umm Kulthum's ensembles and other singers from that era.

In the culture of Quran recitation, the slow *tajwīd* art of the likes of Mustafa Ismail continues officially every Friday, just prior to the weekly sermon, where a famous reciter will read for 30-40 minutes in this style. Aside from this, there also emerged schools and specialists who teach young Quran memorizers, with the musical gift, to recite Quran in the style of one of the giants of the Golden Age. One prominent teacher who recently passed away is Ahmad Mustafa Kamil, a prodigy student of Mustafa Ismail.

Before continuing, we need to highlight the difference between two different approaches to the art of Quran recitation. The terms *tartīl* and *tajwīd* are overloaded terms in Islam and Muslim culture. In the former, they refer to the science of Quran recitation. Specifically, *tajwīd* is the 'science of giving every Arabic letter its due' and includes various subdisciplines, such as *makhārij al-hurūf* (vocal pronunciation of letters), *sifāt al-hurūf* (characteristics of letters) and others.

From this perspective, *tartīl* is simply 'reciting Quran according to the rules of *tajwīd*'. However, in Muslim culture, gradually throughout the 20th century and coinciding with the Golden Age, *tajwīd* and *tartīl* came to also signify two different styles of Quran recitation. *Tajwīd* refers to the slower melodic and *maqām* conscious style of recitation, like Mustafa Ismail's, whereas *tartīl* refers to a recitation style with quicker tempo that is often used in prayer. Hence, one finds recordings of the entire Quran described as either *Mushaf Murattal* or *Mushaf Mujawwad*, meaning either quicker or slower tempo, respectively.

However, in both the *tajwīd* and *tartīl* styles of recitation, the actual disciplines of *tajwīd* and *tartīl* that we mentioned above apply, with the additional study of *maqāmāt* for those interested in the *tajwīd* style of Mustafa Ismail and others. What emerges over the decades leading to the 21st century is that *maqāmāt* became the exclusive propriety of the *tajwīd* school of recitation, including those young reciters today who are invested in imitating Ismail and others from that era. On the other hand, the culture of *tartīl* recitation, by and large, lost its *maqām* consciousness.

In contrast to the *sammī"a* of Ismail and Umm Kulthum, many listeners of Arabic music today or Quran recitation cannot tell the difference between the various *maqāmāt*. I often receive recordings from friends who say at the outset: "Please listen to this reciter, his recitation is so beautiful!" And I can guarantee almost 99% of the time, they will be reciting in one *maqām*, *kurd*. This *maqām* is so overused that I quickly turn off any reciter once I detect he is reciting in this *maqām*.

The use of *maqām* is not merely about having a beautiful voice or hitting all the right notes in the scale of the *maqām*, especially as pertains to Quran recitation. As I show in my study of Mustafa Ismail's melodic narrative, the brilliance of reciters like him was in their ability to utilize *maqāmāt* accordingly to reflect and augment the emotional power of the verses they are reciting. Ismail used a somber *maqām* like *sabā* to convey sadness and then immediately modulated to *maqām 'ajam* to reflect joy and God's alleviation of difficulties.

Meanwhile, reciters today use *maqām kurd*, which evokes melancholy, to recite all types of verses, about hell, paradise, expansion, constriction all the while completely disregarding the emotional content of the verses. This is all the result of the loss of *maqām* consciousness, as I mentioned above. More importantly, this is not a deterioration only in the culture of Quran recitation, but also in song and music. One can find a similar loss in other aspects of musical composition as well, most notably the inability to utilize complex rhythm signatures, unique to Arabic music, and relying instead on overused tempos like 4/4 or 2/4.

Here, we need to tether our earlier discussion of the advent of Wahhabism to the destruction of music as a medium of storytelling in Muslim cultures. As we have seen, the Golden Age of Arabic music was catalyzed by the likes of Uthman al-Mawsili, a Quran reciter from a bygone era. Even Umm Kulthum, who would eventually become – and remain – the first lady of Egyptian music, began as a young singer in a family of religious chanters. In other words, the Golden Age of Arabic music owes its success largely to the heritage of musical progress developed under the auspices of Muslim culture prior to the 18th century.

And so, what happens when such a genealogy of musical production, theorization and practice is suddenly halted, as happened at the hands of Ibn 'Abd al-Wahhab? The first aftermath is obvious: the absence of musical instruments and dearth of musicians. But remnants from the old order remain, and they migrate here and there and continue teaching, as al-Mawsili did. However, it becomes considerably more difficult to propagate one's knowledge to the younger generation, especially if teachers like al-Mawsili were to remain in places where this prohibition against music was rampant.

Later, something else happens, namely that society at large no longer contributes to the growth of the craft of music and loses the ability to recognize and engage with its language meaningfully, which we have described as *maqām* consciousness. This is what yields the inability of most of the Quran reciters today to recite in any other *maqām* than *kurd* or to even know that they are reciting in this *maqām* or what a *maqām* is to begin with. Over time, with the prohibition against all artforms, as occurred with Wahhabism, the society loses their very aesthetic sensibility and sensitivity.

This phenomenon is eloquently described by the Iraqi Palestinian novelist Jabra Ibrahim Jabra:

> I don't like those naive ones who graduate with high marks, specializing in the sciences, but don't listen to music, don't know a single poet or even watch a single film. They never

> tried to write a poem or mix colors together to draw a painting.
>
> I don't understand these people who lack any private rituals, bereft of mannerisms and details. They don't care about the colors of their buttons, the texture of wood on benches. They are satisfied with any red-hot drink and care not for the flavor of tea.
>
> Life is in feelings, details and taste … it is to sway your head in joy, sadness or ecstasy while listening to an old song. That you react to the smell of jasmine as it breezes from an ancient street near the first town square.

Wahhabism might have ushered in a movement of outward religiosity, but at the expense of spirituality, creativity and being human.

And so, with this new world order, by and large, becoming a religious Muslim meant listening and reciting the Quran, not music. Meanwhile, the arts became largely the exclusive propriety of the secular class. All of this would gradually change after September 11th and the Arab Spring series of revolutions in the following decade, whence forth the younger Generation Z found that the religious conservatism of the previous century was no longer a viable means for engaging with the world.

What this meant for Islam's contribution to the arts generally and music specifically is that one can no longer find a Farabi, Kindi or Ibn al-'Arabi today who practices, teaches or contributes to the craft of music from within and motivated by Islamic spirituality. Unsurprisingly, these figures and their works have themselves been deemed heretical. Across American mosques today, a preacher can get in a lot of hot water for mentioning Ibn al-'Arabi or Rumi. Trust me, I know from personal experience.

Among many of my own oud teachers, those who happen to be Muslim, I cannot find one who espouses their craft as being harmonious with the current state of Islamic practice or creed. Actually, by and large, one finds that the largest contribution to Arabic music today comes not from Muslims, but rather Arab Christians who have long held a status as custodians of this craft, even in premodernity. Today, the Palestinian virtuoso Simon Shaheen stands as one of the most consequential masters of Arabic music, in both the Arab world and specifically the United States.

As he himself mentions, when he moved to the United States in the 80s, this artform was known as cabaret music for belly dancers. It was regarded seriously neither academically nor classically. Hailing from a musical family, Simon learned both the oud and violin at a very young age at the hands of his father, the musical master Hikmat Shaheen. When he moved to the United States, he completed a graduate degree in the Manhattan School of Music and later at Columbia University. Most importantly, Shaheen single-handedly introduced Arabic music, as a serious discipline, in North America and internationally.

Once appointed as professor of strings at the prestigious Berklee College of Music in Boston, Shaheen has had a few major contributions – among many – worth mentioning. First, he created the first annual retreat on Arabic music that has graduated countless musicians who are now accomplished performers and teachers at this very retreat. Second, he facilitated virtual auditions for prodigy musicians from Palestine who have received fully paid scholarships and who now perform as leaders of bands and ensembles across the United States, one of whom is my dear friend and brilliant Qanunist Firas Zreik.

Thirdly, he started the band Qantara that has composed and released many albums since 2000. Simon's contributions cannot be overstated, for he is not a single musician with many albums who knows how to play the oud and violin well. Rather, Simon Shaheen is a leader of a cultural movement. He facilitated the introduction of Arabic music into Western culture, not only through his own works, but also his many students who now continue his work as well as pave their own way forward.

But one may ask: how does Simon Shaheen, a Palestinian Christian, fit into this overarching narrative about Islam and musicality? Precisely because he is a carrier of a heritage that was shared among Muslim and Christian Arabs. When one listens to the recording of Shaheen performing Darwish's *Zuruni*, one hears a modern rendition of a song written and taught to Darwish by a Quran reciter, al-Mawsili. More than that, as Simon himself told me, he was invited to the sacred city of Sufism, Konya, to perform alongside Turkish oudists like Mehmet Bitmez during the annual Semazen ceremony of the whirling dervishes.

Not to mention that Shaheen as a master of *maqām* is also well-versed in the musicality of Quran recitation. During one of my conversations with him, he advised which reciters to listen to and from which era. Here, I also need to emphasize that Simon's homage to the cause of his people and the ongoing suffering in Palestine is a powerful embodiment of what we previously described as the potency of art as resistance against injustice and oppression. Simon might not voice his opinion politically, but he does something which I believe is more effective: he humanizes Palestinians, as more than just victims, but as musicians and artists, which is not part of the mainstream portrayal in the media.

But where does all of this leave the sacrality of music and sound in the heart of Islam today? The reintroduction of musical practice among Muslims, since the Wahhabi onslaught, has taken some time. As I mentioned above, much changed after September 11th and the subsequent decade's Arab Spring, when the younger Generation Z found the apolitical and asocial religious fundamentalism of the past no longer a viable means for existing and functioning in a new world order.

When the discomfort with music and the arts slowly disappeared, it did so mostly among Muslims who practiced or had some form of affiliation with Sufism. This includes both *tarīqa* (path) Sufism or those who sought the individualized approach of *tazkiya* (self-purification), as propagated by the likes of Hamza Yusuf in America. However, in both instances, there was always a laden fear and anxiety that music and the arts can corrupt, if one is not careful. And in many

Sufi *turuq* (sg. *tarīqa*), music and the arts are still as forbidden as in Wahhabism.

The journeys of musicians who converted to Islam, like Cat Stevens (Yusuf Islam), is emblematic of the angst surrounding the arts. Soon after converting to Islam, Stevens left his guitar for decades. He continued to sing various religious odes and even recorded recitations of the Quran. But it was only recently, perhaps in the last two decades, that he picked up his guitar again and even sang some of the great classics which he had recorded prior to conversion, such as *Father and Son* and others.

Young Muslims today, many of whom look up to Yusuf Islam, such as my dear friend and brilliant musician Alman Nusrat and others who attend my workshops on Islam and creativity, find themselves returning to their passions of guitar, oud, poetry or comic book art decades after being told it was *harām* (forbidden) by an uncle at their local mosque.

This was the status quo I had known until I accompanied the Sufi master and contemporary saint Mawlana Shaykh Hisham Kabbani in 2015. What I realized soon after meeting and befriending some of his closest *murīdūn* (sg. *murīd*, disciple) was a unique relationship between master and disciple where Shaykh Hisham not only tolerated art practice and cultivation among his students but guided them through their crafts. I discuss this in detail in my earlier work, *A Nostalgic Remembrance*.

One of these students is a jazz musician and longtime *murīd* of the guide, LuFuki who graced this work with one of the two forewords at the beginning. LuFuki and his partner Tazeen Ayub perform together in an internationally renowned jazz band, *Divine Providence*. Prior to any concert, LuFuki always puts a small picture of his guide atop one of the amplifiers on stage. This is a symbolic move highlighting a deeper reality, that both LuFuki and Ayub receive divine knowledge and guidance from Shaykh Hisham through the very plucks of their strings.

Other disciples of Shaykh Hisham founded the *Reed Society for Sacred Arts* that regularly hosts renowned Qawwali musician Dhruv Sangari (Bilal Chishti). Their deep investment in music reveals another tutelage and spiritual guidance from Shaykh Hisham. During one meeting, these students highlighted that every Sufi master receives communication from God through one of the five senses, then channels that knowledge to their students.

Then, they stated that Shaykh Hisham had spoken of the Quranic verse: "Hold on together to the rope of God and do not separate" (3:103) as a reference to vibrations of the Divine Voice and primordial creative command: *Kun* (Be!), with which we began this chapter. This manifests clearly in the countless musicians among Shaykh Hisham's disciples, as well as those of his guide, Shaykh Nazim al-Haqqani. Jazz musicians like LuFuki and Ayub, religious singers like Anwar Barrada or guitarists turned lutists like Mason Zantow regularly visit the lodge and perform on its premises.

There are other Sufi groups in America that espouse such a musical aura, namely the Inayatiyya, named after Hazrat Inayat Khan whom we mentioned previously. This 20th century sitar musician turned Sufi mystic in the Chishtiyya order was sent by his guide to spread Islam in the West through music. Eventually, as stated previously, his teachings in the groundbreaking work *Mysticism of Sound and Music* found their way into the private library of almost every major jazz musician in America, from Miles Davis to Yusuf Abdul Latif and John Coltrane.

And indeed, one can certainly consider Coltrane's legacy and the current Church of St. John Coltrane in San Francisco to be an unfolding of the summit of metaphysics in sound and music in Islam. Various opinions even contend that Coltrane's masterpiece *Love Supreme* is a guise for *Allah Supreme*. Coltrane, Yusuf Abdul Latif and their contemporary inheritors such as my friend LuFuki present a viable and living translation of a metaphysics of sound and music from Shaykh Hisham Kabbani's teaching and even preceding Khan's work, tracing its lineage all the way back to the time of Ibn al-'Arabi.

But what distinguishes the Inayatiyya from Mawlana Shaykh Hisham Kabbani's Sufi *tarīqa*, the Naqshbandiyya, is that the latter is considered one of the more conservative Sufi paths. Other branches of this order, such as the Naqshbandiyya Mujaddidiyya prohibits musical instruments altogether, like many other orders. In this regard, Shaykh Hisham followed in the footsteps of his own guide, Shaykh Nazim al-Haqqani who reformulated the Naqshbandiyya into a new branch, Naqshbandiyya Haqqaniyya, that is uniquely positioned to spread Islam in harmony with the modern world.

And this is where the sacred image of sound and music in Islam finds itself today, dispersed in various directions, some outwardly Muslim and others less so and others still non-religious or secular. And perhaps, this is the ideal way in which this heritage can exist in a globalized world where religious formalities have run their course and people increasingly seek meaning liberated from form. However, what remains to be clarified – in the next chapter – is a flavor of the expansive metaphysics of sound and music and how that can be dressed in various garments (e.g., secular, religious, etc.) in today's world.

Metaphysics

The first movement of love from us to Him was through sound
— Ibn al-'Arabi, *The Meccan Openings*

We return to the origin, *Kun* (Be!) with which God began creation in the Islamic mythos. For Muslim saints, this is the pre-eternal, eternal, incessant and continuous source for all sound and music in the universe. It is a moment that remains outside of time; rather, it is the very birth of time itself. In turn, all voices, sounds and music that espouse beauty stand as a reminder and remembrance of that ancient memory, as Habib Umar b. Hafidh mentions in the quote with which we opened the previous chapter.

Among all the Muslim saints throughout history, perhaps none has written so extensively about experiential metaphysics as Muhyiddin Ibn al-'Arabi, known as *al-Shaykh al-Akbar* (The Greatest Master). Born in Murcia, Spain in 1165, Ibn al-'Arabi lived in Andalucia during a period described as 'Convivencia' (co-existence), when Christians, Jews and Muslims lived together and where motifs from the three faiths migrated easily among all three communities. This reveals itself clearly in Ibn al-'Arabi's writings where, like a *bricoleur*, he weaves a new spiritual tapestry from not only Islamic sources, but also Neoplatonism, Christianity, Judaism and various other sources.

Already in his teenage years, he experienced mystical visions and began secluding himself at the local cemetery in Seville, where he saw 'Isa b. Maryam (Jesus son of Mary) in a waking vision. He spent the next two decades traveling across Iberia, North Africa and later, around 1200, migrated eastward towards Cairo, Baghdad, Hebron, Anatolia, Mecca and Medina before finally settling and passing away in Damascus in 1240. As James Morris highlights, Ibn al-'Arabi's contributions have such a lasting impact on subsequent Islamic thought, all of which may be considered a mere endnote to his teachings.

He is also considered one of – if not – the most prolific Muslim polymaths, authoring around 280 works often while traveling. Two of these monographs stand above all others: *al-Futūhāt al-Makkiyya* (The Meccan Openings) and *Fusūs al-Hikam* (Bezels of Wisdom). Spanning over 6400 pages, the former work is a voluminous encyclopedia of experiential metaphysics, which Morris calls *tahqīq* – itself a key term in Ibn al-'Arabi's writings. The latter is a shorter work of around 200 pages, yet most authoritative in Islamic history.

Well into the 18th century, one is hard pressed to find a Sufi text that has received more commentaries than the *Bezels*. It was a mark of authority and legitimacy for any Sufi mystic to author a commentary on this work. More importantly, by tracing the genealogy of these commentaries, one realizes the full extent of Ibn al-'Arabi's influence on Islam and Muslim culture. For instance, the commentary of Dawud al-Qaysari was instrumental in shaping the Ottoman educational system at the hands of authorities like Mulla Fanari.

Further eastward, the commentary of 'Abd al-Razzaq al-Qashani would reach Mughal India and shape the court of the ruler Akbar and his ecumenical project known as *Dīn al-Haqq* (Religion of the Real). Meanwhile, further east, 'Abd al-Rahman Jami's commentary on the *Bezels* in Farsi helped Chinese Muslim scholars Liu Chih and Wang Tai Yu introduce Islam to China in a neo-Confucianist light[5], while Hamza Fansuri utilized these various commentaries and Ibn al-'Arabi's own works to establish a distinct metaphysics of Islam in the Malay Archipelago.[6]

In other words, since Ibn al-'Arabi's time, there is no Islamic civilization or culture that does not owe its efflorescence, at least partially, to his legacy. This is due not only to how much he has written or the depth and complexity of his writings. Rather, there is a unique universality and creative spirit in his language that renders his teachings attractive to seekers, both Muslim and non-Muslim. Indeed, it is a testimony to this liberated approach that most of his readers and those interested in his teachings today are either non-Muslims or Muslims at the margins, those deemed 'non religious' by

---

[5] See Sachiko Murata, *Chinese Gleams of Sufi Light*.
[6] See Sayyid Naquib al-'Attas, *Mysticism of Hamza Fansuri*.

the mainstream Muslim community.

Throughout my work over the past two decades, teaching about the sacred role of creativity in Islamic spirituality through the lens of Ibn al-'Arabi's metaphysics, I have found that it is specifically artists, both Muslim and otherwise, who are not only most attracted to his teachings but also most capable of comprehending him. I am convinced this is due to the fact that he was himself an artist of sorts. The sacred scripture and other Islamic or non-Islamic sources, as well as the entire cosmos, was a palette for Ibn al-'Arabi to paint his canvas of experiential metaphysics.

This is supported by the statement of Shaykh Hisham Kabbani: "It is not enough to know Arabic to understand Ibn al-'Arabi. One must be a poet to understand him." This is one of the reasons why I authored my previous work, *A Nostalgic Remembrance: Sufism and the Breath of Creativity*, as well as this book, focusing specifically on the metaphysics of sound and music. In the proceeding paragraphs, I aim to highlight Ibn al-'Arabi's rich exposition and vision of sound and its centrality in his experiential metaphysics.[7]

As expected, Ibn al-'Arabi roots the sanctity of sound and music in the primordial creative command *Kun* (Be!). Which he states was the initial expression of love from God to His Creation. In turn, the first response of love from us towards Him was through listening. In this

---

[7] All the proceeding discussion can be found in the *Meccan Openings* and has been outlined in my earlier paper: "The Divine Audition in the Akbarian Court".

regard, he emphasizes that God always describes Himself in the Quran as "All-Hearing, All-Seeing" and never vice versa. In other words, first comes hearing/listening then sight/vision. This pays homage to Shaykh Hisham Kabbani's own emphasis on the 'rope of God' as a divine vocal cord of vibrations, as well as Habib Umar's rooting of beautiful sounds in the memory of hearing the Divine Voice.

It is worthwhile noting that what Habib Umar is referring to is not only the primordial utterance *Kun* but another audition, when God "took the covenants from the children of Adam: 'Am I not your Lord?'" (7:172). In both instances, sound has the primacy. Ibn al-'Arabi emphasizes that this original creation is not a historical beat in the past. Rather, all things are recreated at every moment. Thus, *Kun* is an incessant Divine Utterance. Actually, it is the same original *Kun* that continues to reverberate and echo until the end of time.

This is because, as the Prophet Muhammad ﷺ stated in a *hadith*: "God was and nothing was with Him, and He is now as He has always been". And so, all created things experience the original *Kun*, which Hazrat Inayat Khan refers to as *sawt sarmad* (primordial sound), at every moment incessantly. One can say that this utterance and the involuntary *istima'* (attentive listening) of all things to it is the very meaning of life. Ibn al-'Arabi also tells us that this creative command is like water, transparent in itself but shaped by the color of its container.

Ibn al-'Arabi often quotes the 10th century Muslim saint al-Junayd in this regard, who stated when asked about *ma'rifa* (gnosis) that: "The color of water is the color of its container." And so, Ibn al-'Arabi states that "abodes have their rulings." After the creative command is uttered, it descends to the Divine Throne, at which point it separates into either an *amr* (command or prohibition) or *khabar* (news). The *amr* descends further to reach the Divine Chair and differentiates into *wājib* (obligatory), *mandūb* (recommended), *mubāh* (permissible), *makrūh* (detested) or *harām* (forbidden), while a *khabar* separates into *mādī* (past), *hādir* (present) or *mustaqbal* (future).

It is at this moment that Ibn al-'Arabi states that the first instance of *tarab* (musical ecstasy) emerges in creation, when the Divine Throne is moved into joy due to the overwhelming power of the creative command. It is from this initial intoxicating experience that all other instances of *tarab* are born. Stated differently, all instances of *tarab* experienced by human – and other – beings in the universe are mere mirror reflections of this initial ecstasy.

This emanative – read 'Neoplatonic' – vision of the cosmos is foundational in Ibn al-'Arabi's writings, where he recurrently portrays the physical world as a mirror reflection of the spiritual realm. Later commentators in the Akbarian school, such as Sa'id al-Din Farghani outline five stations in *marātib al-wujūd* (levels of being): *lāhūt* (divinity), *malakūt* (spiritual realm), *jabarūt* (imagination), *nāsūt* (physical world) and *al-insān al-kāmil al-tāmm* (the perfect and complete human).

The complex and sophisticated nature of these levels are too consuming to discuss here, but we state that the *tarab* of the Divine Throne occurs in the level of *malakūt* (spiritual realm) and is thenceforth mirrored and projected in each of the lower levels of being (imagination, physical and perfect human). However, this also means that this *tarab* originates in the Divine Essence. For God is the creator of all things and nothing can exist without first having a root in His Will and Decree.

The origin of *tarab* in the Divine Essence manifests as Divine *farah* (joy), as the Prophet Muhammad ﷺ states in various teachings. God laughs and is happy when human beings perform various acts of goodness. And just as our first interaction with God is listening to His Creative Command *Kun*, so does He also listen to us. As a matter of fact, Ibn al-ʿArabi pushes this reflective process between God and human beings to its utmost limit: we are His mirror reflection, in every possible way.

The Andalusian mystic excavates the shape of this reflexivity from the analogy of the mirror. He states that just as our reflection in the mirror is inverted (e.g., if we move our right arm, our reflection moves its left arm), so are we also inverted reflections of God. This manifests in the fact that God's inward Essence never changes but His outward *tajalliyyāt* (Theophanies) are never the same, as the Quran states: "Every day [moment] He is in a different affair" (55:29). Meanwhile, our inward spiritual states are always in fluctuation, while our outward form is more stable and constant.

This also manifests in the acts of speech and listening. Ibn al-ʿArabi states that every human being is either a *muhaddith* (speaker) or *muhaddath* (spoken to). If we wish to speak to God, He will listen, but if we wish to hear His response, we have to be silent. But since God has already described Himself as *al-Sami'* (the All-Hearing), who hears all things all the time, then that must mean that all created things are speaking to Him every moment, whether we realize it or not. Similarly, His Divine Speech never ceases, and so we are also constantly listening, whether we realize it or not.

Ibn al-'Arabi also distinguishes between Divine *Kalām* (Speech) and *Kalimāt* (Words, sg. *kalima*). The former he regards as eternal and uncreated, while the latter are "God's created things which never cease or expire." The proof for this distinction is in the Quran. The Andalusian mystic states that if God had manifested to Mary with His Speech, as He did to Moses, she would have perished. Rather, He cast only one of His Words, Jesus, whence she was able to carry the Word in her womb.

Ibn al-'Arabi continues to highlight that if each of the created things is a word, then a sentence is a day in our life while a page is a stage in our maturity. Meanwhile, a chapter is the life of a human being while an entire book is the lifetime of a community or society. This imagery is also Quranically rooted: "On the day that We fold the heavens and earth like the folding of a book." (21:104). And yet, he also states that Jesus is both a single word and many words, since the Quran describes Mary as "believing in the Words of her Lord" (66:12).

Jesus is a single word from the perspective of his essence but many words from the perspective of his different limbs and aspects. Also, in relation to Christ, Ibn al-'Arabi beautifully highlights the etymological relationship between *kalima* (word) and *kalim* (wound); God's Words imprint themselves on the canvas of creation just as pen wounds a paper. As a Muslim saint, Ibn al-'Arabi might not believe in the crucifixion OF Jesus, but he hold that the son of Mary IS himself a spiritual crucifixion, an embodiment of the way that God creates all things.

Here, we are also drawn to highlight that although *kalām* (speech) is one of God's essential attributes, *Mutakallim* (Speaker) is not one of the 99 *al-Asmā' al-Husnā* (God's Most Beautiful Names). Ibn al-'Arabi addresses this indirectly in the *Meccan Openings* when he describes each of God's Names as a source of inspiration for one of the crafts. Unsurprisingly, He regards the Name *al-Bari'* (The One who Gives Form) as the source of inspiration for painters and architects. However, for poets and orators, he regards the Name *al-Basīr* (All-Seeing) as the source of their inspiration.

All this alludes to an important point: God's Speech is His Creative Power. His Words are the visible created things that fill the canvas of creation. God Speaks, and from His Speech emerges all the visible creation. God never ceases to speak, and we never cease to listen. But since we are His Mirror reflections, Ibn al-'Arabi also states that God's Attributes of Listening and Speaking harmonize with our outer forms and essences, respectively. The former never cease praising Him, while the latter are always silent, listening to Him.

In the *Meccan Openings*, the Andalusian mystic beautifully pushes this description of creation as God's Words to its limit. He focuses on a common term in the Quran, *'ibra*, which means parable. He states that the entire cosmos is a matrix of *'ibārāt* (sentences) over and through which we must perform *'ubūr* (crossing over) from the body to spirit and form to meaning. Behind the form of each the Words in existence is the meaning at the side of God. Ibn al-'Arabi also poetically regards this visible cosmos as *majāz* (metaphorical) that alludes to *al-Haqq* (the Real).

Before making the transition from speech to music, let us tie a few loose threads regarding Jesus, as the Word of God, and poetry. Ibn al-'Arabi places various knowledges in each of the seven heavens where a prophet resides. The order of these prophets mimics the Prophet Muhammad's ﷺ *mi'raj* (ascension journey), when he met, in ascending order: Adam, Jesus and John the Baptist, Joseph, Enoch, Moses, Aaron and Abraham in each of the spheres respectively. This is also the sequence which Ibn al-'Arabi experiences during his own spiritual ascension.

He then states that one can find in the second heaven of Jesus and John the Baptist the source of the knowledge of poetic meters and oration, undoubtedly in relation to Jesus' status as the Word of God. But here we also find a subtle connection to God's Creative Power. During his ascension, Ibn al-'Arabi asks John the Baptist why he resides with Jesus in the same heaven. The prophet states that this is due to two reasons. They are cousins and the spirit, represented by Jesus who is described in the Quran as a 'spirit from God', never separates from life, represented by John the Baptist, whose name in Arabic, *Yahya*, means the one who lives.

Ibn al-'Arabi states that wherever the spirit is found, life is surely there as well. And so, just as Jesus and John are historical cousins, so is the spirit and life also metaphysically related. And since Jesus is the Word of God and a spirit from Him, then the Words of God and His Speech are also tethered to life. This is also why Ibn al-'Arabi situates the ancient knowledge of semiology, or affecting change in the world through speech, in this second heaven. Christ not only embodies the miracle of Divine Creativity, but also how God creates through Speech.

And since God's Words are His Creation, filled with life and spirit, Ibn al-'Arabi tells us that there is naught in this creation that is mute. Even the inanimate objects are in constant speech, as we mentioned above, from the perspective of their outer forms, while their essences are forever silent and in *istimā'* (attentive listening) to their Creator. This is, unsurprisingly, Quranically rooted: "There is naught a thing save that it glorifies His Praise, yet you do not comprehend their glorification." (17:44).

In another verse, God also states: "Have you not seen that all that is in the heavens and earth glorifies God and the birds are in groups, each has known their prayer and glorification." (24:41). There are two important points here. First, these Quranic verses are identifying the incessant speech of all created things as Divine Praise. The second verse specifically states that each created thing already knows its appropriate prayer and praise. This might be understandable in the case of birds or animals, but what about human beings, some of whom do not even believe in God?

Ibn al-'Arabi states that the limbs and bodies of disbelievers do indeed praise God, even their tongues as well, despite the fact that the people do not consciously praise Him. For just like Jesus, each limb of the human being (e.g., tongue, hands, feet) is a word with its own life and spirit. The harmony and balance occurs when the involuntary speech (praise) of our body coincides with our voluntary glorification of Him. However, the question remains: how do we each know our unique praise if some of us never even believe in God?

In this regard, Ibn al-'Arabi states that knowledge is not a process of learning something new but rather remembering what we have forgotten. This is why the Quran states, regarding disbelievers: "Do not be like those who forgot God, whence He caused them to forget their own selves." (59:19). In other words, Ibn al-'Arabi holds that those who claim they do not believe in God have simply forgotten the primordial covenant. They, like all things, have heard His Voice but can no longer trace its memory.

Another important topic related to forgetfulness of this primordial sound is loss of understanding of the cosmic sound. Both Ibn al-'Arabi and the 18th century Moroccan Muslim saint 'Abd al-'Aziz al-Dabbagh discuss this from different aspects. The Andalusian mystic explores this in relation to the term *bahīma* (pl. *bahā'im*), or four legged beasts. Ibn al-'Arabi foregoes this literal understanding of the word and creatively tethers it to the phonetically related term *mubham* (obfuscated). In turn, he states that animals are called *bahā'im* because they communicate with God in a *mubham* tongue which arrives to their beings from the Divine Presence of *bahamūt* (obfuscation).

Meanwhile, al-Dabbagh explores this in relation to infants, whom he says are born speaking the language of the spiritual world, which adults cannot comprehend and thus deem as gibberish. Al-Dabbagh even states that *gāgā*, for example, is actually the name of God in the spiritual realm and *mūmū* is the word for water in that sphere as well, which children say often. The reason why infants are made to speak this language, al-Dabbagh explains, is that their memory of the spiritual home is still intact. If they were to utter these secrets in a tongue that adults understood, the latter would lose their minds.

As infants grow older and gradually lose their memories of the unseen, they begin to speak normal adult speech, which al-Dabbagh states is a corruption of the tongue of the spirit. Here, an anecdote that I heard directly from a Sufi saint is in order. There was a town with a tall wall, behind which lay a complete mystery. Every once in a while, somebody in the town tried to climb and look behind the wall, only to jump to the other side and never return.

One day, a man from the town told the people that he will climb the wall and tie a rope around his waist. If he tries to jump over the wall, they should pull him down. The man surely tried to jump over the wall and when the townsfolk pulled him down and asked him what he saw, they found that he had become mute. The question is: did the man become mute because the townsfolk were not supposed to learn what he saw or because all of human language was incapable of describing what he saw, thus it was pointless for him to speak?

Al-Dabbagh explains that the corruption which has occurred to human language over time is due to the distance and forgetfulness of our spiritual origin. Specifically, he states that our current speech wastes many letters. Whereas the spiritual word for water is *mū*, one syllable, the Arabic term is *mā'*, which is three letters. In other words, only one of these syllables, the 'm' sound indicates water spiritually, whereas the other two letters are wasted. Thus, modern language has lost the eloquence of its ancestor, the spiritual tongue.

All of the preceding paragraphs deliver us to an important question: how do we transition this entire discourse regarding the sacrality of divine and human speech to music in Ibn al-'Arabi's writings? The answer is simple: the Andalusian mystic himself states that music is the ancestral language. He instructs us to consider the letters of the alphabet, which are pronounced at particular points in our vocal system. Each of these letters is nothing but sustained sound that is disconnected in particular places and altered in pitch or tempo.

Ibn al-'Arabi also offers an extensive insight into the life inherent in these letters of the alphabet, the building blocks of human language. He regards them as 'one of the nations which God has created' that, as we mentioned above, have their 'own prayer and praise'. Here, Ibn al-'Arabi is building on his earlier presentation of God's Words as the created things. Likewise, the letters of the alphabet make up the words of human speech, that we create through our breath, just as God also creates through Breath.

He then describes the 'life and spirit' of this human language. He states that letters are like the skeleton; when they come together, they become like flesh. Then, accents and diacritics dress them in skin, hair and eyebrows. Finally, when the human breath flows through them, it brings them to life just the Divine Breath, which Ibn al-'Arabi calls *nafas al-rahmān* (Breath of the Most-Merciful) fills the human body with spirit and – in turn – life. Interestingly, here we find a correspondence between Ibn al-'Arabi and al-Dabbagh, since both mystics trace an ancestor for human language.

Whereas the former regards music as this original tongue, the latter regards the language of the spiritual realm as the progenitor. And yet, there is immense overlap between these two visions, namely that for both mystics, music and the tongue of the spiritual realm are more eloquent than spoken language, which Ibn al-'Arabi states directly in the *Meccan Openings*. Also, for both mystics, this original tongue is simpler, with less wasted syllables, than its current descendant. Perhaps, then, music is this very language of the spiritual realm which al-Dabbagh speaks of.

Beethoven certainly would agree, since he states that "the vibrations on the air are the breath of God speaking to man's soul. Music is the language of God. We musicians are as close to God as man can be. We hear his voice, we read his lips, we give birth to the children of

God, who sing his praise." And Mawlana Shaykh Hisham Kabbani, who regarded the rope of God to be the reverberating cord of Divine Speech, would agree with Beethoven.

Here, an interesting connection emerges between music and the prophet David for Ibn al-'Arabi. As the Quran states, God taught David "wisdom and most eloquent oration" (38:20). Biblically, of course, David is known as the 'Great Musician'. This characterization is reinforced by the Prophet Muhammad ﷺ who praised his companions who recited the Quran with a beautiful voice by telling them: "You have been gifted a reed-flute from among those given to the people of David." In turn, Ibn al-'Arabi states that the psalms of David were not revealed in spoken language, but rather music.

Perhaps, the *fasl al-khitāb* (most eloquent oration) which David was taught by God is this craft of music, which the Prophet Muhammad ﷺ then tethered to Quran recitation. If Ibn al-'Arabi holds that music is more eloquent than spoken language, and the Prophet ﷺ compares the beautiful voices of his companions in Quran recitation to musical instruments, reed-flutes, then what effect or importance does melody have on the meanings of the Quran? Let us not forget the *hadith* of the Prophet ﷺ from the previous chapter: "They are not from us those who do not melodiously recite the Quran."

Let us return to the notion of *tarab*, which originates in the ecstasy of the Divine Chair as it receives the Divine Creative Command *Kun* and its differentiation into an *amr* (command) or *khabar* (news). As stated previously, Ibn al-'Arabi holds that this primordial *tarab* descends and emanates into each of the lower levels of being (imagination and the physical realm). He states that the sound and melody born out of musical instruments originate in the *tarab* and music of the *aflāk* (planetary orbits). Actually, the music we hear from musical instruments is not produced by the wood, according to Ibn al-'Arabi, rather the very rotation of these heavenly spheres.

In order to appreciate the manifestation of *tarab* inside human beings, we must first understand Ibn al-'Arabi's vision of our species. Inheriting the concept of *microcosm/macrocosm* from Greek philosophy, most probably through Neoplatonism, the Andalusian mystic regards the human being as a mirror (microcosm) of the universe (macrocosm). This is actually attributed to the Prophet's cousin, Ali b. Abi Talib in a verse that can be found in his *diwan*: "The sickness and cure is within you. You assume yourself to be something small, while the entire universe is enfolded within you."

Ibn al-'Arabi takes this analogy to its utmost limit, whereby all that exists in the universe, the macrocosm and larger human being, necessarily also finds its reflection within us. Thus, he states that the cosmic planets and stars represent our five senses, while angels and spiritual beings represent our inner faculties of imagination, rationality, reflection and memory. Meanwhile, our heart is a mirror of prophets and messengers whom God sends to guide His Creation.

In turn, the *tarab* that originates in the Divine Chair and moves the planetary orbits into ecstatic movement also reflects in our own inner orbits, which are the five senses. Here, Ibn al-'Arabi's notion of *hayra* (perplexity) comes into play. In the *Bezels of Wisdom*, he states: "Reality is perplexity. Perplexity is anxiety and movement, and movement is life." Ibn al-'Arabi is unique among Muslim saints in his emphasis on this paradox and agitation as a destination on the path.

Elsewhere, he also states: "From the darknesses of ignorance to the light of guidance and darkness of perplexity." Thus, he distinguishes between the darknesses – plural – prior to belief and the darkness – singular – that is higher than simple faith and which the seeker must attain in order to arrive at a state of bewilderment in God's Presence. This is also supported by a *hadith* where the Prophet Muhammad ﷺ is narrated to have said: "My Lord, increase me in perplexity regarding You." However, our interest is regarding the association of perplexity with movement.

In the Quran, God speaks of the sun that it "sprints towards its *mustaqarr* [place of stillness]. That is the decree of the Most-Exalted and All-Knower" (36:38). Remarkably, the Quran also speaks of a *mustaqarr* [place of stillness] inside each human being: "And He is the One who molded you from one soul, whence it has a *mustaqarr* and vessel. We have delineated the signs that they might comprehend" (6:98). In other words, both the sun and human being are – or should be – in constant movement until they reach their *mustaqarr*, place of stillness.

When the sun reaches this destination, it dies. And so, all living things necessarily move as a sign of life. Both movement and the spirit are inseparable from life. More importantly, the *tarab* which the sun experiences manifests in this agitation and perplexity that moves it to sprint across the cosmos, effusing the light and heat necessary for life on earth. Each of us also should journey in our own orbit, moved by the *tarab* of incessantly hearing the Divine Address and being agitated into perplexity. For Ibn al-'Arabi, this is the essence of life.

It is indeed remarkable that Ibn al-'Arabi essentially equates *tarab* (musical ecstasy) with life itself. If this musical portrayal is not clear enough, consider that he regards the four strings of the oud as tethered mirrors of the human being's four humors: blood, phlegm, black and yellow bile.[8] It seems that the Andalusian mystic wishes us to perceive the human being, and all of God's Creation, as musical instruments through which He composes the cosmic symphony and all things move in *tarab*, otherwise known as life.

Before departing from this sojourn at *tarab*, I wish to highlight a slight comparison between Ibn al-'Arabi's and Hazrat Inayat Khan's respective visions of the relationship between sound and form. The latter asks in the *Mysticism of Sound and Music*: "Why is music called the Divine Art? [Because] sound alone is free from form." On the other hand, Ibn al-'Arabi holds that God speaks form into being. For the Andalusian mystic, music is the ancestral human language,

---

[8] During Ibn al-'Arabi's time, the oud had only 4 strings, whereas currently there are 6 pairs with a drone as the 7th. Some oud designs have even more strings.

rooted in the realm of spirits, and is what gives birth to form.

Of course, one may clearly talk about form in a musical sense, such as the form of rhythm, melody, phrasing etc., which Khan also highlights regarding the poetic and musical structure of the universe whereby rhyme and meter govern our daily life in the form of a dance between night and day, repeated seasons and even our alternating steps while walking. However, for Ibn al-'Arabi the material realm not only mimics sound and music but it is born of Divine Sound and Music. The entire visible cosmos is a matrix of God's Words that He Voices into being.

Let us transition to the notion of *samā'* (auditory session) which as I explained in the introduction is a term related to the title of this book and also a central theme in Ibn al-'Arabi's discussion of the sacredness of sound and music. The first mention of this term in the *Meccan Openings* occurs while the author is discussing a specific rank of saints known as the 'poles of intention', who are "concerned with knowledge of intentions because they looked at the Word and knew that its letters were not brought together and harmonized save for a structure that signifies a meaning."

Ibn al-'Arabi tethers the form of the Word to its meaning. As he also states elsewhere, each of the alternating shapes that any given Arabic letter takes, depending on its place in a word, has a different spiritual power. He then continues that "these men do not prefer *al-samā' al-muqayyad* [limited auditory sessions] through *naghamāt* [melodies]. Instead, they advocate for *al-samā' al-mutlaq* [unbounded auditory sessions] that affects the understanding of meanings and is *al-samā' al-ruhānī al-ilāhī* [spiritual divine listening]."

The Andalusian mystic distinguishes here between two modes of *samā'* (listening) to music: one that is bound to melodies and another that is tethered to meaning. Although it seems that he offers a drastic and abrupt differentiation between these two modes of listening, he later clarifies and presents a more nuanced approach. Already in the second mention of *samā'*, Ibn al-'Arabi tethers *anghām* (sg. *nagham*, melody) to spiritual states and not mere emotions. This is found during one of a few explorations of the *mi'rāj* (ascension) journey in the *Meccan Openings*.

The Andalusian mystic holds that *samā' al-alhān* (listening to melodies) puts human beings under the influence of *al-ahwāl* (spiritual states) that descend upon listeners from the *aflāk* [orbits], as we mentioned above, "whose movements generate *naghamāt tayyiba* [sweet melodies] which ears find amiable." Remarkably, Ibn al-'Arabi then describes the microcosmic mirror of 'sound to form': "Then, the soul of the listener is attached to either a maid or young man. On the other hand, if they are from the people of God, then their attachment will be to the imaginal love of Divine Beauty."

Whether it is an image of a human beloved or Divine Beauty, sweet melodies for Ibn al-'Arabi must necessarily give rise to form in the imagination of the listener. Thus, just as the macrocosm is a matrix of God's Words that He Speaks into being, so does the music the human being hears also give birth to forms in the imagination. The human being is a mirror, not only of the universe but also God. Ibn al-'Arabi relies upon the *hadith* where the Prophet ﷺ quotes God as saying: "I am at My Servant's opinion of Me" to reiterate this point time and again in his writings.

In the third mention of *samā'* in the *Meccan Openings*, where the author describes our initial movement of love towards God as a result of hearing the Divine Command *Kun*, he explains that "this is why we sway and feel moved during *samā' al-naghamāt* [listening to melodies], due to the Word *Kun* that emanates from the Divine Form in the unseen and seen. For just as *Kun* has two letters, *kaf and nūn*, so does the world also have two realities, outward and inward." Ibn al-'Arabi continues to lift the source of *anghām* (melodies) and music to a higher realm, not only to the degree of spiritual states, but now the primordial Divine Creative Command.

More importantly, he tethers the movement of swaying, which is indicative of *tarab*, as a projection in us of the same ecstasy experienced by the Divine Chair. Interestingly, Ibn al-'Arabi uses a similar image as 'swaying' to also describe the ecstasy which the Prophet ﷺ experienced when he entered the Divine Presence during his *mi'rāj*. Later, he returns to this connection by highlighting that "God said: 'He is the All-Hearing and All-Knowing' and 'All-Hearing and All-Seeing'. Thus, He prioritized hearing above knowledge and vision."

He continues to state that this priority which the Name *al-Samī'* (All-Hearing) has above other Names is due to our very coming-into-existence that occurred because of hearing the Divine Command. In turn, every physical sway and movement of ecstasy that we experience when listening to melodies and music is an embodied remembrance and homage of our birth into being. This is why Ibn al-'Arabi unequivocally states that "every *samā'* [audition] that does not result in ecstasy and a 'coming-to-be' is not, in reality, an audition."

Thenceforth, the Andalusian mystic differentiates between three types of *samā'*: divine, spiritual and natural. The first pertains to Divine Secrets and involves hearing from all created things and through everything. The reason for this, as explained previously, is that "in the perception of these listeners, all things are the words of God that never perish." As for the spiritual audition, "that is attached to the movement of the Divine Pens in the preserved tablet of existence. Indeed, the entire creation is an unfolded scroll, and the cosmos is an exposed book therein."

This is yet another layer of *tarab* in the spiritual realm, pertaining to Divine Pens in the higher spheres. Ibn al-'Arabi then returns to the four humors of the human body that find a reflection in the four strings of the oud and unveils their higher order: "Since audition is based upon four pillars: essence, relationship, direction and expression, both the spiritual and divine auditions are also based upon four: essence, Divine Hand, Pen and their movement. Likewise, the natural audition is also based upon the four elements [water, earth, fire, air] and in this manner the human form is molded."

We now transition to the last and perhaps richest discussion of melody and *samā'* in the *Meccan Openings*. This emerges whilst the author is discussing the subtlety of breath. As we mentioned previously, Ibn al-'Arabi regards the Divine Creative Command *Kun*, which God Speaks through *nafas al-rahmān* (Breath of the Most Merciful), to be like water, quoting al-Junayd, namely that it takes the shape and color of its container. This is also his focus in this excerpt.

He states that "it is impossible for subtlety to become density, since realities cannot change. However, what is subtle can become dense, just as what is hot can become cold and vice versa." This is all to clarify that "spirits are naturally subtle, but once they are embodied, they become dense. Likewise, bodies are naturally dense, but once they change in form, they become spiritualized and veiled." The connections here abound, specifically the homage to Jesus who is described in the Quran as a 'spirit from God' and is created through breath.

Both the spirit and breath are like water: shapeless and colorless yet bound by their abodes and containers. Ibn al-'Arabi states that this phenomenon is "most visible among musicians. For sound, as it is, cannot change, but the musician can make it low and high to affect the listeners towards happiness, joy, expansion, sadness or constriction." And so, Ibn al-'Arabi indirectly adds sound to the same tier as breath and spirit and regards it as a subtle reality that is bound by its various abodes and containers.

Then, he states that "the path of the musician is to understand the hidden meaning in God's statement: 'Our utterance to something if We will it', for this is also the intention of the musician, to utter: *Kun!* They do this by composing speech from sounds that affect their listeners." It is amazing that Ibn al-'Arabi places musicians at such a high status, as did Beethoven, where they constantly weave a remembrance of the primordial memory *Kun* through sound and melody.

He ends this discussion by offering a poignant analogy between musicians and cats: "Do you not notice how a cat does not speak like humans yet makes various sounds when it is hungry so that its owners know when it needs to eat?" Ibn al-'Arabi and al-Dabbagh find common ground once again, for the latter also recounts the story of a saint who experienced an overwhelming *fath* (spiritual opening) when he witnessed a cat cleaning itself; how and why did he perceive God in this animal, he could not explain, but he did.

Similarly, Ibn al-'Arabi wants us to appreciate the sounds a cat makes to indicate hunger, happiness, sadness or anger as *mubham*, obfuscated and beyond the expressive ability of human speech. Yet, we understand it intuitively. Sound generally, and music specifically, work in the same way. We comprehend and process music spiritually, not rationally. For Ibn al-'Arabi, this is not a matter of psychosomatic dimensions, but rather primordial metaphysics. We sway in ecstasy when we listen to music and its melodies because all things do, inwardly and outwardly, all the way up to the Divine Throne.

This chapter presents us with a nuanced overview of the sacredness of sound and music in Ibn al-'Arabi's metaphysics, but perhaps what emerges out of this entire discussion that is most poignant is that the tongue of the spiritual realm, and perhaps God's Speech also, is music itself. It is not surprising to hear a musician like Beethoven say this, but it is rather extraordinary – and jubilant – to witness such a testimony from a Muslim saint like Ibn al-'Arabi.

Why has God chosen music as His medium? Why is His First movement towards us one of speech and ours towards Him of listening? Because, clearly, sound is the most expressive and primordial communication. Of course, one could say that sound is as such because God has chosen it. Nevertheless, the mystery of its primacy still emanates in sparks and glimpses all around us. Sound, and its most eloquent manifestation, music, gives form to meaning and meaning to form.

As we transition to the next, and final chapter of this book, we sojourn with all that we have discussed thus far in a contemplative space to weave our own reflections on the sacredness of sound and music. The proceeding pages are fermented thoughts that have fomented for a decade in my heart and mind, ever since I picked up the oud in 2017. But prior to this, I would like to offer a short primer on Arabic music and the *maqāmāt* (modalities) system, since many of my reflections are refractions on these modes and their itineraries.

A Primer on *Maqāmāt*

A maqām is nothing but intervals.
If the intervals are not maintained, there is no maqām.
— Simon Shaheen

There are much better books that explain *maqāmāt* in detail, perhaps the most important, and recent, is *Inside Arabic Music* by Johnny Faraj and Sami Abu Shumays. There are also countless websites and videos on YouTube by masters of Arabic music who dive into this deep ocean, of which Simon Shaheen has exclaimed that we have barely scratched the surface. Notable examples of these resources include, but are not limited to, Maqamworld.com and Musiqana.net.

However, given that in the final chapter of this book, *Reflections*, I offer my own meditations on Arabic music and *maqāmāt*, I decided that it would be prudent to include a simplified understanding of this artform, especially for the Western reader or musician who is more familiar with concepts like major and minor scales or the circle of fifths. Of course, in the proceeding I'm indebted to all the teachers I have mentioned in the acknowledgment, specifically my own oud teachers Omar Abbad, Tariq al-Jundi, Simon Shaheen, Ahmad al-Khatib, Tarek Abdullah and the exceptionally talented teacher of *maqāmāt* Sherif Hussein, whose videos on YouTube have allowed me to introduce *maqāmāt* in a simplified manner to Western musicians over the past few years.

Paraphrasing Faraj and Abu Shumays, a *maqām* is a melodic itinerary that depends less on the starting point (tonic) and, as both Shaheen and Hussein emphasize, more on the *ab'ād* (intervals) between the various degrees of the *maqām*. Prior to visualizing this musical narrative, I would like to provide a brief history on the development of Arabic music throughout the last two centuries, since that influences our presentation of the topic in this primer.

Prior to the 20th century, Arabic music was transmitted orally, much like all knowledge was generally conveyed in the Arab and Islamic world in the past. Arab musicians rarely if ever used sheet music to record or teach their works to students. This is also influenced by the fact that classical Arabic music has always been – and remains – largely improvisational. One can notice, for instance, the remarkable absence of music stands or sheets in Umm Kulthum's ensembles during her two-hour concerts.

Often, the *sitt* (lady, an honorary title for Umm Kulthum) would rehearse a song with her ensemble and composer for months prior to performing it onstage. By that time, the ensemble would have already memorized the piece, leaving the door open for the audience to request repetitions of entire phrases, which they often did. In other words, it was a practical impossibility for any of the musicians to follow sheet music, since that would hinder the improvisational spirit of the performance.

Also related to this improvisational spirit is the fact that every musician in this genre has a responsibility to flavor a musical word, sentence or phrase with their own *zakhārif* (ornaments). In turn, even now when Arab musicians increasingly rely upon sheet music, the written notes remain mere guidelines for the musician to build upon and interpret the music based on their style and emotion. Many have highlighted this similarity between Arabic music and jazz.

As a result of the *First Congress on Arabic Music* that took place in Cairo in 1932, much of the orality of musical transmission in Arabic music changed, to accommodate a cultural communication between Arabic and Western music. Here it is worthwhile noting that Western music had, at this point, also gone through various reformations and developments. Most notable among these is the standardization of the tuning frequency of musical instruments in the West to A4=440Hz.[9]

Up until the 19th century, many of the European countries had their own tuning standards. For instance, France introduced A4=435Hz in 1859, while Italy adopted 440Hz in 1885, soon to be followed by the United States in 1917 until the *International Organization for Standardization* set 440Hz in the 1950s. The purpose behind this procedure is to allow a collaboration between musicians across

---

[9] A4 refers to the note A above middle C (C4) on the piano. By setting A4 to 440Hz, the rest of the keys on the piano can be set accordingly.

Europe and North America, which was difficult to accomplish when each musician in an ensemble is playing according to a different tuning.

The standardization of all instruments to 440Hz was not accepted by everyone. Even in the 20th century, not only Arab musicians like Farid al-Atrash or Riyad al-Sunbati, but even Western ones like Jimi Hendrix, Coldplay and Metallica continue to incorporate older standards (e.g., 432Hz) in their music. However, whereas Western musicians have relied upon sheet music for many centuries, Arab musicians did not, and so these drastic reforms, ushered by a Western impetus, had tremendous repercussions on understanding, performing and teaching Arabic music.

My first exposure to these different tuning standards was when I listened to Farid al-Atrash's famous improvisational piece, *taqsīm al-rabī'*. When I tried to play the piece from sheet music, I noticed that it sounds much higher in pitch than Farid's, even though I was playing the same notes. This is when my teacher Omar Abbad informed me that Farid tunes his oud one whole note below 440Hz, which is the 392Hz standard. Since trying this new tuning, I have never set my oud otherwise.

Thus, whereas nowadays the Arabic note *rast* is often equated with C4, that was not always the case. *Rast* could be slightly lower or higher depending on the *maqām* and the emotional preference of the musician. Unfortunately, many students of Arabic music no longer know these Arabic/Farsi names of the notes and consider teaching this heritage to students of Arabic music as an 'unnecessary difficulty'. However, I am convinced that Arabic music is not only the final product, but more importantly the history and story behind the music.

I would like to introduce the names of the musical notes in Arabic, for two reasons. First, I refer to them recurrently in the final chapter, *Reflections* and, second, I am emotionally invested in referring to these notes by these names as a means of preserving this heritage. The range of notes that have specific names in this system usually range from what has been standardized as G3 (G below Middle C) to C6 because this is the usual range of sound employed in Arabic music and which accommodates the central instruments in the Arab ensemble, namely the oud, also known as the 'king of the Arabic music ensemble'.

But prior to sharing the names of these notes, it is worthwhile highlighting an important difference between Arabic and Western music, namely microtonality. Simon Shaheen describes this as an imaginal red key between each white and black key on the piano. Here, however, matters are also oversimplified. This is because, traditionally, the note *sīka* for example, which is now standardized to E4 half flat fluctuates between a slightly higher frequency, such as in *maqām sīka* or *rast* for example, or a lower frequency, like in *maqām bayātī*, all of which we will discuss momentarily.

I mention this precursor to explain the abundance of notes in Arabic music, whereby between each pair, for instance C and D, there are 4 possible standardized degrees: C, C half sharp, C sharp/D flat, D half flat and D. For this reason, Simon Shaheen states that Arabic music does not need to rely on harmony as much as Western music since there is an abundance of possible sounds and notes to use on the oud or any other fretless string instrument.

You can find the names of these degrees below. Please note that not all the tones are notated since they tend to follow the same naming convention as the others, whereby a half sharp is called *nīm* and half flat is *tīk*. Notes in the first octave are usually prefaced with *qarār* (base) while those in the second octave are described as *jawāb* (response), highlighting the conversational nature of Arabic music.

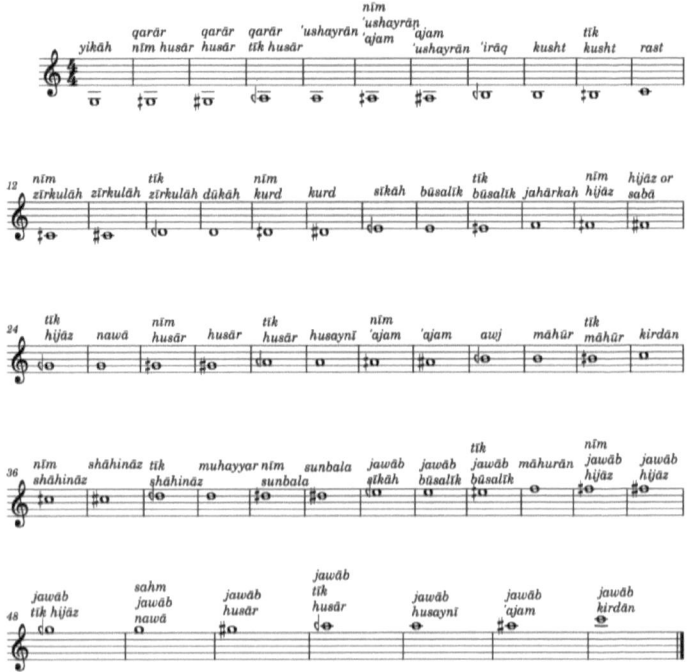

A Primer on *Maqāmāt*

We now transition to the *maqāmāt* by beginning from Western music as the — unfortunate — reference, simply due to the aforementioned standardization. Nevertheless, this will help simplify understanding the nature of *maqāmāt* as an itinerary, as opposed to a static musical scale akin to western music. Of course, the proceeding discussion is in no way comprehensive, but rather an introductory outline to what Simon Shaheen has described as the deep ocean of Arabic music.

Let us begin with the C major scale, which looks like this:

In western music, this and all other major and minor scales are regarded as a single unit of 8 notes. However, let us reimagine this scale as two sets of notes conjoined together:

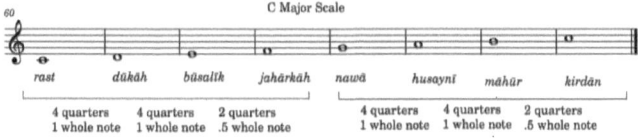

What we find is that the C major scale actually consists of two sets of tetrachords (4 notes): C4 to F4 and G4 to C5. Moreover, in terms of the *ab'ād*, or distances between the notes, these two tetrachords are exactly identical. The intervals in the first set are 1 whole interval followed by another whole interval followed by a half interval. Alternatively, counted in quarters since Arabic music is microtonal, the distances are 4 quarters, 4 quarters and 2 quarters.

This interval arrangement, (4,4,2), is what we call in Arabic music a simplified *jins* (genus) *'ajam*. Thus, a C Major scale basically consists of two sets of *jins 'ajam* conjoined by a whole interval between F4 and G4. This appendage that connects the two *ajnās* (sg. *jins*) is called a *bu'd mukammil* (completing interval). Moreover, the lower *jins*, in this case from C4 to F4 is called the *jidhr* (root) that decides the family of the *maqām*, while the upper *jins*, known as the *far'* (branch) distinguishes a relative in the same family.

Therefore, a C major scale is one variation of *maqām 'ajam*. More importantly, all major scales can be seen as transpositions of this same *maqām*. Therefore, we call G major *'ajam* on *nawā*. However, since the C major scale in this *maqām* presentation is no longer a static unit of 8 notes, whereby we have a degree of freedom at the inflection point, known as the dominant tone, or *ghammāz* in Arabic, which in this case is G4, we are able to derive more relatives from the family of *'ajam* by changing the *far'* (branch) of the *maqām*.

For example, here we have a relative in *maqām 'ajam* known as *shawq afzā*, where the branch is not a tetrachord, but rather an *'iqd* (pentachord or 5 note set) known as *nikrīz*:

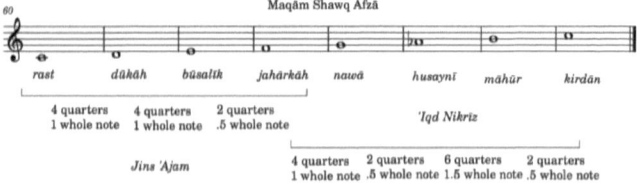

Here, the inflection or modulation point has changed somewhat from G4 to F4, whereby there is no longer a 'completing interval' between the root *jins 'ajam* and branching *'iqd nikrīz*. Therefore, when a musician is composing or improvising in *maqām 'ajam*, the itinerary or melodic narrative begins with the root *jins* then travels into either *jins 'ajam*, *'iqd nikrīz* or any of the other relatives in the *'ajam* family. This is precisely why a *maqām* should be regarded as an itinerary, not merely a static scale.

This itinerary trait of *maqāmāt* manifests clearly in the improvisational genre of *taqsīm* in Arabic music, which can last anywhere from 1 to 10 minutes. A *taqsīm* has three stages: *istihlāl* (preamble), *naqla* (modulation) and *qafla* (closure). In the first, the musician introduces his audience to the *maqām* family in which they wish to improvise, as listeners become aware whether the musician wants to explore *'ajam*, *rast*, *hijāz*, *bayātī*, *nihāwand*, *sabā* or *sīkāh* which are the seven – but certainly not all – major *maqām* families.

During this stage, the musician should exhaust the possible phrasings and words in the *jins* of the *maqām* they wish to improvise in. Then, in the *naqla* (modulation), they begin to journey and explore some of the relatives in this melodic family. Thus, for instance, in the case of *'ajam*, a possible itinerary in the *naqla* stage would be to explore both *jins 'ajam* and *'iqd nikrīz* in the branch. In a similar fashion to the *istihlāl*, the musician here also explores as many phrases as possible in order to give the relatives of the *maqām* their due right.

Thenceforth, in the last stage, the *qafla* (closure), the musician returns home to the root *jins* – or *'iqd* or even *nisba* (trichord) – of the *maqām*. The audience should not be deserted in the middle of the *taqsīm*. A story should have been told that is understood melodically. In some instances, a musician will switch the entire family of the *maqām* during the modulation stage, but only temporarily, before returning to the original family. This requires mastery, which Riyad al-Sunbati had and does during his improvisation in *maqām hijāz*.

With this in mind, I would now like to introduce all the major *ajnās* (sg. *jins*, tetrachords), *'uqūd* (sg. *'iqd*, pentachords) and *nisab* (sg. *nisba*, trichords) of the major *maqāmāt* families:

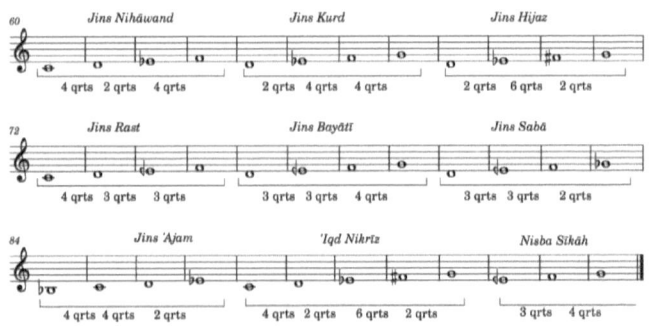

A few words are in order here. I have transposed *jins 'ajam* in the above from C4 to B3 flat, which is called in the Arabic notation *'ajam 'ushayrān*. The reason for this change is that *maqām 'ajam* in Arabic music is more commonly played on this degree than C4 (*rast*). Here, an interesting piece of information emerges: the names of the notes in this Arabic notation often refer to the *maqām* that has an *irtikāz*

on this note, or where the note is the tonic. Thus, C4 has been standardized as *rast* because *maqām rast* is often played from this degree.

Of course, that is not to say that other transpositions of *maqām rast* are not possible. On the contrary, one often finds *rast nawā* (*rast* transposed to G4) in many compositions or *bayātī husaynī* (*bayātī* transposed to A4).[10] It is a tricky business trying to ascertain whether these names refer to a note or an entire *maqām*, but this was never an issue between musicians in the past, who digested the melodic narratives of *maqāmāt* orally.

Thus, each of the above *ajnās*, *nisab* or *'uqūd* delineates a different *maqām* family. Considering the limitation of space, I will not include the notations of all the relatives in each *maqām* family. Instead, I include the following table with each family, at least two of its relatives and what the branching *jins*, *'iqd* or *nisba* is therein:

Family	Relative 1	Relative 2
'Ajam	'Ajam 'Ushayrān Jins 'ajam + jins 'ajam	Shawq Afzā Jins 'ajam + 'iqd nikrīz
Nihāwand	Nihāwand Jins nihāwand + jins kurd	Nihāwand Murassa' Jins nihāwand + jins hijāz
Kurd	Kurd Jins kurd + jins nihāwand	Lāmī Jins kurd + jins kurd
Hijāz	Hijāz Jins hijāz + jins nihāwand	Shāhināz Jins hijāz + 'iqd nikrīz
Nikrīz	Nikrīz 'Iqd nikrīz + jins nihāwand	Nawā Athar 'Iqd nikrīz + jins hijāz

---

[10] As opposed to *maqām bayātī husaynī* which is a relative in the *maqām bayātī* family.

Rast	Rast	Sūznāk
	Jins rast + jins nihāwand	Jins rast + jins hijāz
Bayātī	Bayātī	Bayātī shūrī
	Jins bayātī + jins nihāwand	Jins bayātī + jins hijāz
Sabā	Sabā	
	Jins sabā + jins hijāz	
Sīkāh	Sīkāh	Huzām
	Nisba sīkāh + jins rast	Nisbah sīkāh + jins hijāz

As mentioned above, the list provided in this table is hardly exhaustive, for some *maqām* families contain as many as 10 relatives while others, like *sabā*, barely contain two, only one of which I have included above. Another crucial point is that certain *maqāmāt* have different names when transposed. For instance, *maqām huzām* is called *rāhat al-arwāh* (tranquility of souls) when transposed to B3 half flat (also known as *irāq*), and as one of my teachers Dr. Tarek Abdullah informed me, it is not entirely correct to regard *rāhat al-arwāh* as a mere transposition of *maqām huzām* since it has a different melodic itinerary than the latter.

Other notable examples include *maqām shad 'arābān*, which is *maqām shāhināz* in the *hijāz* family transposed to G3 (*yikāh*). Likewise, we have *maqām sultānī yikāh*, which is *maqām nihāwand* also transposed to G3. Also, many of the *maqāmāt* mentioned above have not only two conjoined *ajnās*, *'uqūd* or *nisab*, but rather many interlocking parts. A case at point is *maqām sabā*, which includes *jins sabā*, *hijāz* and *kurd* overlapping at various degrees.

More than that, the ascending and descending degrees of any given *maqām* often change. For instance, while exploring the ascending scale of *maqām nihāwand*, one usually plays the normal *nihāwand* from the table above, but while descending – such as during a *qafla* (closure) in a *taqsīm* – a musician will explore *nihāwand murassaʾ*. In other instances, such as in *maqām sabā*, the second octave of the *maqām* changes entirely from *jins sabā* to *jins hijāz*. To accommodate this, the tonic of the second octave changes from D4 (*muhayyar*) to D4 flat (*shāhināz*).

Why all of this complexity and variation? For a very simple reason: because Arabic music was and remains an improvisational artform. The different ascending and descending scales of a *maqām* allow for variation in the various stages of a *taqsīm*, as does the alteration of the second octave or transposing the *maqām* altogether to a different tonic. And even with all these mechanisms, the possible phrasings remain ultimately under the jurisdiction of the musician, their mastery, style and emotional state.

A testimony to the oral richness of this tradition is that a Quran reciter like Mustafa Ismail never formally studied *maqāmāt*, yet as I show in my research titled "The *Maqām* Narrative in Mustafa Ismail's Recitation", he follows the trajectory of the *taqsīm*, mentioned above, over the course of 1 hour and 40 minutes. This in addition to his own unique modulations and phrasings that cannot be found elsewhere.

When musicians and quran reciters in Egypt want someone to improvise musically, they simply ask: "*Qūl hāga*", which translates literally to: "Say something!" This is a testimony to the metaphysical reality of music as a primordial tongue, that 'language of God' as Beethoven describes. As we transition to the next and final chapter of this book, I hope to bring together all the various threads of the preceding pages into a series of meditations on the sacrality of sound and music, not only as a spiritual journey to God but also a mirror that reflects back to us the answer to an important question: "What does it mean to be human?"

Reflections

Whatever color and words cannot describe, music can
– Hazrat Inayat Khan

This chapter, I hope, will be what the Quran describes as *majma' al-bahrayn* (the meeting of the two seas): the fresh water of metaphysics, salty water of history and the *barzakh* (liminal interstice) in between, which is my own meditation on this artform of sacred sound and Arabic music. Over the past decade, this journey has overwhelmed me with emotion and creativity; I finally feel confident I have arrived at the shore of my craft.

Throughout my life, I have journeyed through many crafts, from filmmaking in high school and college, then creative writing in Arabic and English as I began my doctoral journey with Ibn al-'Arabi, only to finally find my creative home with the oud, Arabic music and the art of *maqāmāt*. And yet, when I at last arrived at this shore, I realized it has been there all along. It is as Steven Spielberg said, while praising composer John Williams, that "often, you might even leave a film that John Williams has scored, and a week later you may forget the film, but you will never forget the music."

I often find myself, when thinking about my favorite films and tv shows, that what lingers or catches me into the world of the story is the music. And as Ibn al-'Arabi has shown, the ancestor of speech and writing that continues to gaze and testify from the beyond is pure unmitigated sound. In other words, despite my meandering around all different artforms, what I have been actually seeking is sound. I am reminded of something powerful which Spielberg's friend, George Lucas said: "I wanted to be an anthropologist, filmmaker and work for National Geographic. But I realize now that no matter what I would have done, I would have ended up doing *Star Wars* anyway."

I will share a series of numbered meditations on the previous chapters, bringing them together in a synthesis at the interstice. As I often state: somethings need to *foment* before they *ferment*. The reflections I am sharing here have written themselves in my heart over the past decade, long before I allow them the chance to breathe before you, as ink on paper. I am convinced that this is a responsibility of every musician and artist who is passionate about their craft: to share their own ruminations on the journey and what God has revealed to them. As the Muslim mystic Abu Madyan used to say: "Don't give us 'so and so said', but rather what has arrived in your heart!"

1

Let us begin as we did the previous two chapters, with *Kun!* How does this manifest in the oud, guitar, piano, cello or violin? Where does the *sawt sarmad* (primordial sound) emerge for the musician?

How does each note plucked from the string relate to that first ancestor? What about a word, phrase, sentence, composition or corpus of works?

Whatever we heard on that day of covenants, it remains as a dormant memory, waiting to be reactivated through remembrance. But both the memory and remembrance are sounds, so is the entire affair not music?

What is a musician trying to reach as they expend countless notes and shed an immense amount of sound? As they leave one work behind and begin working on the next one, are they haunted by drafts and the ghosts of previous sounds?

Perhaps every musician extinguishes countless tones to remember but one note, which they heard as *Kun*. They are trying to 'come to be' by reaching a goal in the distance, only to discover it is here and now.

As Ibn al-'Arabi says, the gnostics see only One behind the forms of all annihilated words of poets and artists. The artist calls it women, men, status, wealth, power or fame. But it is He who veils Himself behind the form, only to become more present in hiding.

The Prophet ﷺ secluded himself in the cave and received revelation. Then, he had to go down the mountain to convey what he had heard. The same movement occurs during his *mi'rāj*, ascension.

He leaves the city of his birth, Mecca, towards Medina only to return later on towards the closure of his mission. The journey proceeds in cycles, one begins a new rotation once the old has culminated.

As the Prophet ﷺ himself said during his last sermon: "Time has cycled in its original form on the day that God created the heavens and earth."

Hazrat Inayat Khan says that the musicality of the cosmos manifests in its repeating rhymes and rhythms. And so, the universe is a song with a repeating chorus and interchanging verses.

But what is the ascension of the musician? What is their *hijra* (migration)? What cave do they seclude themselves in during their silent dance of sound?

Perhaps they seclude from their own selves. They remain silent, with eyes closed, as their hands speak with string and pick. It is a wondrous affair, how a musician speaks so eloquently while silent.

If there was ever a beautiful *fanā'* (annihilation), it is a musician who speaks loudly while intentionally ceasing to exist. But such is all art, as a film director told Jack Lemmon: "Do less!"

3

The Prophet ﷺ instructed that "they are not from us those who do not melodiously recite the Quran." He also said: "God listens more attentively to the reciter with a beautiful voice than one of you listens to their instrument" and "beautify the Quran with your voices."

What power does melody hold over meaning? Is it ornament, decoration or mere embellishment? What is missing from the Word when the melody is absent?

To ask this is to question whether a body can live without a soul, for is human speech, that utters the Quran, not itself a child of music? How can we disown the ancestors of our sound?

Why does Ibn al-'Arabi hold that speech dancing with melody moves us more than just words? Perhaps melody is the very key to unlocking meaning?

Maybe meaning is not bound by grammar, but rather begins at its threshold, just as learning how to paint starts with holding a brush, learning perspective or shading.

As my oud teacher Tariq al-Jundi said: "Knowing the grammar of a language does not make one a poet." Melody, in turn, is as Rumi described: "Beyond belief and unbelief there is a field, I will meet you there."

Melody is proof that speech and language point to the beyond.

4

Once, the Muslim caliph sent an army with one soldier, al-Qa'qa', whence the generals complained: "What will one soldier do?" The caliph responded: "He is worth a thousand!"

Why was al-Qa'qa' worth a thousand? Because of his voice. He yelled *Allahu Akbar,* and the walls of the fortress fell. As my guide Habib Umar said: "You might think you are pious, but can your voice even move a napkin?"

What barriers can our sounds sunder? What walls does a musician try to pierce in a composition? Are we aware of the hurdles or is it more important to just focus on the integrity of sound and music?

If music is the ancestor of language, then what epics are we weaving through melody and which darkness are we confronting on the cliffs of clefs?

Between every crescendo and glissando, what is happening to the protagonist and antagonist in our story? And if music is far more eloquent than words or colors, what are these characters and settings saying in pure sound which they cannot otherwise?

Perhaps what is more important than all of this is to simply find our inner al-Qa'qa' and channel him with all might and honesty in the story, so that we do not break the walls without, but within, between the silence of the notes.

5

The Prophet ﷺ praised his companions who had a beautiful recitation of the Quran by comparing their voices to a reed-flute from among those give to the people of David.

Al-Farabi considered the human voice to be the greatest instrument. And it is indeed a wondrous tool, since it is both a wind and string instrument. And yet, many who believe in God believe musical instruments are not allowed.

I often wonder about birds and other animals, what they might think of those human beings who assume that this primordial language is forbidden by God?

"Do they not see how the camel was created?" God asks. As Ibn al-'Arabi states, the camel is a *bahīma* (four-legged beast) that speaks in a *mubham* (obfuscated) tongue.

And so, perhaps God is asking us: "Have you not listened to the ancient language spoken by animals so that you might remember?" We have not only forgotten but also forgotten how to remember.

But here is the more important question, what is our inner reed-flute through which we can melodiously give life to meaning? Perhaps it is not a physical instrument but a state of musical being whence we speak and peak at our utmost eloquence.

Fortunately, this is also a prophetic inheritance from David!

6

So many have wondered about the *maqām Muhammadī*, or the modality in which the Prophet ﷺ recited Quran. What does his melody sound like, coming from the heart upon which scripture descended?

Some have theorized it is closest to *maqām jahārkāh*, a relative in the family of *maqām 'ajam*. But perhaps it is at the intersection of all *maqāmāt*, or maybe a dance between all of them.

Ibn al-ʿArabi states that scholars inherit the prophetic actions and statements, while saints inherit prophetic states and breaths. Unsurprisingly, states give birth to actions and breaths breathe statements.

Thus, perhaps what is more important than wondering about the *maqām Muhammadī* is to hear his voice ﷺ directly. His melody is still reverberating in the ether of every oud, reed-flute and every musical instrument.

And perhaps, if you can trace the fragrance of his breath, then you can know all the *maqāmāt* that are cast upon his heart ﷺ. More importantly, do not wonder about the historical *maqām Muhammadī* and neglect its inward mirror within.

"Know that the Messenger of God is within you" Perhaps hearing the *sawt sarmad* (primordial sound) is simply hearing his voice ﷺ, once and for all time.

7

The Prophet ﷺ heard revelation arrive as sound, a prelude to Divine Speech. It came sometimes like the humming of bees, ringing of bells or a metal chain dragged on pebbles.

The arrival of scripture was a divinely ordained creative process. Ruth Stone sees a new novel rushing towards her like a horse galloping down the meadows of rural Virginia.

The Prophet ﷺ is bringing the artist's gaze to this: "Pay attention to how revelation arrives at your heart!" It is not always the same, and with each different sound, something is revealed about you.

Our emotional states are embodied in sound. Fear sounds differently than hope, joy or sadness. As Roland and Bayles emphasize in *Art and Fear*: "The audience of the artist who are not artists are interested in the work, while those who are artists are interested in the process."

And so it is, that the work is the body while the process is the spirit. Knowing the spirit that moves our music allows us to see the narrative of self-knowledge that tethers all the works we produce in our lifetime, as chapters bound by time and spirit.

Most importantly, we need to describe the process as sound first, because that is how we began. First came the sound and listening, then the form and seeing. First comes the humming, then the bees. Let us first hear our inspiration before deciphering what it looks like or what it is trying to say.

8

After the Prophet ﷺ received the first revelation, there was silence for months. He descended shivering and seeking cover from his family. Divine Sound had done all of this.

Do we sense a silence and shiver when we descend from the summit of communicating with God through the language of our craft, especially music?

Between each phrase of music, breath is allowed to breathe in silence. Perhaps a shiver arises when meaning arrives at our skin just behind the speed of sound. How do we feel?

If we do not feel a shiver when we listen to the sound of our passion, is it really our passion? We seek to cover ourselves, fall asleep and hope to process what we heard in the dream world, in imagination.

But in reality, we are trying to return to the realm of reality, where sound came from. We heard a language that our spirits understand had originated elsewhere. Hence, the only way to understand what is being said is to travel to 'elsewhere'.

The silence comes to prepare for a new sentence, to distinguish one abode or state from another. Again: "Know that the Messenger of God is within you", whether you are Muslim or otherwise. Every musician must necessarily experience the shiver and silence of music when they reach the summit.

9

During his *mi'rāj*, the Prophet ﷺ found himself in a place, outside of space and time, of incredible *wahsha* (loneliness). Then, he heard the voice of Abu Bakr, which God informed him ﷺ was an angel in the form of his companion, in order to keep him company.

Souls find solace in the familiar. Ibn al-'Arabi states that God continued to tell the Prophet: "When Moses came to speak with me, he also felt awestruck, whence I reminded him of his staff, and he felt tranquil and confident."

Musicians speak the language of emotions, but how do we process what is familiar to us? What is a familial sound? Is it a melody from our childhood, or maybe a static in the background that signals an origin from a more innocent age?

And what does *wahsha* sound like? Is it just silence, or perhaps an absolute stillness with nothing to process? Beautifully, tranquility and serenity come not from the unknown, but what is homely.

Perhaps, *wahsha* is important for the musician, just so that they are pushed to discover what is familiar and perceive the always expected in exceptional ways.

Again, what is crucial here is that the Prophet ﷺ was relieved from *wahsha* through sound. He did not see the form of Abu Bakr, for sound always has primacy over form, since the days of *Kun!*

10

Whenever the time for prayer came, the Prophet ﷺ would tell his *mu'adhdhin* (caller to prayer) Bilal: "Grant us rest through it [*adhān*] Bilal." Was he saying this about prayer or the *adhān*?

But Bilal did not lead the prayer, the Prophet ﷺ did, so the rest sought must have been through *adhān*. And now we ask, was it the words, voice or melody?

The story of the *adhān* is wondrous. A prophetic companion saw a dream where a Jewish man blew in the horn to signal their prayer, while a Christian man rang a bell, and a Muslim man echoed the formula that would eventually become the *adhān*.

The companion told the Prophet ﷺ the dream and the latter told him: "Tell the words to Bilal and let him recite it out aloud atop of the mosque, for he has a more beautiful voice than you."

Bilal was chosen for his voice, and so perhaps what the Prophet ﷺ sought was not merely the words of the *adhān*, but their dress in Bilal's voice and melody.

I was also moved by the melody of the *mu'adhdhin* in Jordan. I had heard the words before, but the melody brought them to life differently.

Melody unlocks meaning and undocks maladies. And when melody embraces words, it reminds them that they are the child of music.

11

The companion Anas b. Malik recounted the Prophet's ﷺ soft hands and fragrance, whence he could also hear his melody and see his face. The senses of touch and smell help awaken hearing and vision.

Our five senses are partners in a *hadra*, an ecstatic dance of presence. They speak with one another beyond the tongue of the mind. And yet, there is a subtle love between smell and sound.

What is the fragrance of music? Do you smell the breath of wood when you play your violin, oud, guitar or cello? What if you smelled jasmine, rose or musk, whose breath would you be breathing?

Hazrat Inayat Khan had mentioned that the presence of music is right beneath the Divine Essence, and beneath that is the domain of fragrance.

So, I ask: "How does sound translate to fragrance?" Where do they meet? How do they communicate? Both music and fragrance are born from breath, yet how do they understand one another?

And if I smell a fragrance while playing or listening to a melody, what meaning is shared between them, and which can only be spoken in sound vs aroma?

Ibn al-'Arabi says that God speaks to some through sound and others through smell. For those who receive both, God wants them to remember not only *Kun*, but also its fragmented fragrance.

12

The Arabs' mastery over language was almost miraculous. They used the ripples of water to ascertain the rhyme of their poetry. They visualized words as vibrations and waves.

They read verses from left to right as praise, then from right to left as blame. They reversed the time of language, for timelessness was the timeline of the desert.

But I wonder, how did they see language? Did they see words or calligraphy, and did they hear grammar or sound? Where did this infant-like embrace of reality go?

Music teaches us to remember this, to see language as calligraphy and sound prior to words or grammar. The former is seeing language as angels do, while the latter as those who imprison meaning within their understanding.

Ibn al-'Arabi says *ummiyya* (unschooledness) is not about knowing how to read or write but rather relying upon one's heart, not mind. It is learning how to reed before reading.

Perhaps the pre-Islamic Arabs were more affected by the Quran than Muslims today because they knew to first and foremost listen to sound before speech.

Can we resurrect this today? Ja'far al-Sadiq said: "I keep repeating the verses of the Quran until I hear them from the Speaker."

13

The Arabs also had countless words to describe any one thing. A hundred for a lion, two hundred for mountain or river. This is how they boasted to those who thought money is better than the desert.

But I wonder, if the Arabs could do this with spoken language, surely music the ancestor is more eloquent. But how can we say the same thing in a hundred different ways with notes and rhythm?

In Arabic music, *zakhārif* (ornaments) dress the same word in different garments. This is also how Ibn al-'Arabi describes the visits we receive in dreams from spirits.

They have no forms, but they wear garments from our memory to convey a message. They wear a red dress to warn us, blue suit to give us good news or yellow jacket to make us jovial.

Words of music are muses that await our garments of ornaments. A nostalgic phrase in *bayātī* awaits a glissando to make its presence known.

But if *zakhārif* is the dress and body of meaning in music, then our emotions are the spirit. We bring ourselves in silence to each word. Music cannot be cheated, whatever you are will overflow to the top.

As Jesus said: "Every pot flows with is in it", and the same song or sentence in sound will dance differently, once it hears what swells up in the heart of the musician.

The people of Medina were known as *ahl-ghinā'* (people of singing). The Prophet's ﷺ wife had a private singer, and female companions are narrated to have stage names.

Scholars from Medina narrated *hadith* and sang beforehand. Some played the oud, while others considered the sacred moments of *samā'* (listening or playing music) as a time when prayers are answered.

Why specifically Medina? This *sunna* (custom) of beauty seems to be an imprint among its people. The famous jurist Malik b. Anas used to wear his best clothes, put on musk fragrance and burn incense before reciting *hadith* of the Prophet ﷺ.

The people of Medina were disposed to sing, put on fragrance or wear their best clothing before engaging with the Prophet ﷺ, perhaps because he is God's most perfect work of art.

We return to "know that the Messenger of God is within you". Each musician or artist is one of the people of their inner Medina. We pursue beauty at high speeds through our craft.

But we also recognize our need for all the help we can get from all our other senses. We watch film to hear a good soundtrack, look at a painting and listen to the symphony of colors. Beauty begets beauty, and as Ibn al-'Arabi says: "Whoever loves beauty, loves God."

15

Al-Farabi mentions a musician in Medina who wore bells all over his body and could move his limbs in an ecstatic dance to produce any melody he desired.

We dance to music, but what about calligraphy of the body? We dance to music, but what about the embodiment that produces sound? What does a body sound like when it dances in silence?

When I listen to music, I do not just hear the notes, I hear everything else listening attentively. In each note on the oud that is played sincerely, I witness the history of all dance and speech in stillness.

Ibn al-'Arabi witnessed his entire magnum opus in an *elapsed youth* whom he describes in opposites: the silent speaker, simple composite and living dead.

The oud and Arabic music are like this *elapsed youth*. I hear all of time and space collapsing in every cadence. I can hear a *taqsīm* and cry and laugh at the same time.

Such is *majma' al-bahrayn*. The fresh and salty water meet at the *barzakh*, at the liminal interstice which T.S. Eliot calls: "The intersection of timeless with time, an occupation for the saint."

So, how do we witness the dance of our notes? Do we see the pluck of our strings as a knock on the door of ecstasy to open? How many different knocks do we know? The door will open sooner or later.

Al-Farabi also sees *maqāmāt* as children of the night and day. They heal the ailments of body and soul when played at the right time. I wonder which of them is for which moment?

Ibn al-'Arabi also sees all things as children of night and day. Whatever happens during the night, it is their parent and the same for the morning.

Then, perhaps, all things in existence are melodies and *maqāmāt*. But what harmonizes and tethers time and music? Is it only rhythm or is there something more beneath the surface?

Ibn al-'Arabi also tells us that music is the beautiful friction born from the rotation, read 'dance', of the heavenly orbits. But is it not also this revolution that turns night into day and vice versa?

Hazrat Inayat Khan smiles at both Ibn al-'Arabi and al-Farabi as he sees night and day as part of the rhythmic proof that the cosmos is music.

If each *maqām* is a child of night or day, then emotions are as well. Perhaps deciphering which night or day can host the nostalgia of *bayātī* will unveil knowledge of self?

As Ibn al-'Arabi tells us, knowledge of self is to know what each day and night holds for us in happiness, joy, sadness, anger or simply music.

17

Al-Kindi sees music as a door for grace or sin. But it is relational, for a melody that heals the sick is a source of reward, while a sad tune that kills the heart is itself hell.

But perhaps the arrogant need the sad tune, in which case music could be justice. And gifting the sound of joy to the broken hearted is "enlivening all of humanity."

In *Immortal Beloved*, Beethoven states that the waltz makes you dance, and marching band makes you march, music simply puts you in the mental state of the composer.

The Prophet's companion, Abu Bakr, used to instruct when the prayer is called: "Extinguish with your prayer the hell you ignited with your sins."

And so, perhaps the happy melody is itself the paradise for the sick while the tune of the oppressed is the hell of the oppressor. Perhaps music is the musician's bliss.

Likewise, I wonder if music is itself emotion dressed in sound. Perhaps *bayātī* is what nostalgia sounds like when the overwhelming weight of memories becomes too much.

I can almost hear pain scream in *sabā* and feel the complaints of innocence as *hijāz* transitions to *bayātī* in Sunbati's *taqsīm*. But I don't think the emotion is born, I think that is what emotion sounds like.

18

When the Christian troubadours saw Ziryab play the oud, they were inspired to invent the lute, which later evolved into the guitar. The oud embraces both east and west within.

But this was after Ziryab played a happy and sad melody to make the king and his court laugh and cry for 30 seconds each. How did he play? With what emotion? Did he leave anything unsaid or any stone unturned?

Music played sincerely becomes a mirror. It attracts in the silence of performance. Ziryab played for king and peasant alike, and more importantly he played alike for both of them.

For he did not care in whose presence he was when he played, it was enough that he was in the presence of music. He was hearing the primordial *Kun* in every pluck of the string, and made sure his listeners did as well.

Perhaps, then, the troubadours thought the sincerity of the music was in the oud itself, neglecting the marriage of the instrument to the heart of the artist.

But it was a necessary ruse, that allowed them to breathe their own fragrance into the lute. And now the guitar can speak with the same echo but in different hands that carry emotions and memories in incomprehensible tongues for the oud. Yet, the ancestor still witnesses from the beyond.

19

In the Quran, God orders us not only to hear but listen, not only to listen but listen attentively, in silence and stillness, with our entire being.

And if, as the Quran states, that hands, tongues and feet will speak, then they must also be able to listen. For as Ibn al-ʿArabi told us, all things are either speakers or spoken to, but if you can speak then you must also be able to listen for the response.

"If the Quran is recited, then *istami'ū* [listen attentively] to it and *ansitū* [be silent], that you might receive mercy" (7:204). If we are to listen attentively with all our organs, then we can also be silent with all of our being.

But how can we carry this to music? How can we hear God's Speech in the notes? Perhaps we can do this by paying attention to the miracle of the musician who speaks so loudly and eloquently despite their silence, blindness and muteness.

I think a person who simply hears music receives an ambivalent composition, whereas the one who listens hears the words, sentences and phrases. The one who listens attentively hears the alphabet while the who is also silent hears the sound behind the curtain.

Similarly, like Ja'far al-Sadiq, the one who repeats the Quran in the stillness of their entire being no longer hears their own voice, but rather the sound of the Speaker behind the veil, just beyond the vale.

20

Ikhwān al-Safā place music as a foundational discipline in education, as part of mathematics, for it is through music that we understand ratios and fractions.

But is music simply a statistic? Or is it otherwise, that mathematics and all the other disciplines should be embraced as children of music and symphonies of truth in numbers?

How do we appreciate the Pythagorean theorem differently once we know that it is born from the strings of the harp? Do we hear the sounds of numbers and fractions?

The modern man wants to subject all of beauty for the function of utility: music is good if it sells, whereas in the past the best music was often priceless, but both these visions are states of being.

Al-Ghazali says that horses are better than money, because they are praised for their inherent beauty whereas paper money is only worthy for an external utility. If we traded in peanuts, they would be of a higher value than dollars.

Music is inherently beautiful and will always rest as the foundation of all that serves a utilitarian function. Music is not important because it helps us in math and science. Math and science are important because they are born out of music.

At a certain point, we have to decide to be human again.

21

In his *Risala*, al-Qushayri says that only the *fuqarā'* (impoverished) can attain the rank of listening and understanding music. What does impoverishment yield in comprehending sound?

Ibn al-'Arabi poetically said: "Every ship that does not have its own wind is closer to *fuqr* [impoverishment]." But which ship does contain its own wind?

And if He sets you sailing with His Breath, then which horizon is too farfetched for you to reach? Indeed, only the impoverished ships will ever reach their destination.

And so, perhaps the *fuqarā'* who listen to music are those who hear it not from instruments or human musicians, but rather as recurrent sonorous aromas of the primordial breath *Kun!*

This *nafas al-rahmān* (Breath of the Most-Merciful) sets the *fuqarā'* sailing into the horizons of their own being. They hover over waves of their own emotions and reach for islands of gnosis in stormy oceans of sound.

Perhaps, the *fuqarā'* are the only ones who can truly listen to music because they are the only ones who receive it not with their own hearing, but as the musician and instrument embrace it.

The *fuqarā'* learn from the musician how to cease. They relinquish agency and become all ears. Rather, they become music itself.

22

Al-Ghazali famously said: "Whoever is not moved by spring and its roses or the oud and its strings, then their disposition is corrupt and cannot be healed."

Once again, we find fragrance tethered to sound. But al-Ghazali is alluding behind this statement that listening to music is not only a matter of jurisprudence, whether permissible, forbidden or allowed.

Rather, he regards it as an indispensable gauge of our humanity. If not being moved by the strings of the oud means one's composition is corrupt, then what about those who refuse to listen to it?

All things produce sound when they move; isn't it then a sign of death when someone refuses to listen to music? Perhaps the arguments of permissibility or otherwise are denials of this death?

Undoubtedly, you will find that those who refuse to listen to music are not only unmoved by it but are also not musical beings. They lack rhythm in life, harmony in living and melody in movement.

But whereas some musicians are difficult beings, sooner or later they will cry a crescendo that renders their entire faults as a beautiful kintsugi of sound.

Music gauges our humanity. How we engage with sound informs us how much we remember the primordial *Kun!* If those unmoved don't remember, what about those who refuse to listen?

23

Al-Ghazali also said that animals and birds are the only proof needed for the permissibility of music. They sing as speech, and since all musical instruments are designed after animals, they cannot be forbidden.

As I said before, birds must think human beings who do not like music are not normal. They must wonder if we have simply forgotten how to sing or, as Khalil Gibran says, that "singing is the secret of existence."

It is rather a simple, yet deep question: "How can God give us that which He has forbidden? Both a wind and string instrument as our vocal system?"

More than that, God even considers knowing *mantiq al-tayr* (the utterance of birds) as a miracle worth mentioning in the Quran, as a gift that He had bestowed upon Solomon.

Today, much of materialism is disguised as faith. The exile of music is cast in a religious garb, yet it is simpler than that: the human being's loss of the ability to understand what is *mubham* (obfuscated), the language of birds and animals.

But perhaps, if we listened to music more often and understood how different *maqāmāt* convey emotion, we would remember how to speak with birds again. This is why my lovebird always stands on my oud when I start to play.

24

Mawlana Rumi begins the *Mathnawi* by paying homage to the reed-flute's lamentation, its separation from the reedbed, not recognizing it has been elected.

The journey of the reed from reedbed to flute is nothing but utter *sulūk* (journey of self-discipline). It begins with separation from home, what is familiar and familial.

Then, the reed is bent into shape and burnt with fire if need be. Afterall, the pain of *fitna* (tribulation) is what turns dust into gold. The reed is experiencing *tahqīq* (self-realization) of its potential.

Thenceforth, the reed is emptied from the inside, whence all the layers that we once thought were us dissipate. No instrument can produce music if it is not hollow from the inside.

Then, seven holes are made in the reed, symbolizing the opening of the seven *latā'if* (subtleties) or chakras, whence the fingers of the Divine Musician can embrace us through these windows into the unseen.

When our *sulūk* is complete, we become instruments of sacred sound in the hands of the Divine Musician. And like the reed-flute, the Divine Musician is the One who is praised for our performance.

We neither withhold His Breath of Mercy nor the notes He wishes to play.

25

Rumi also told the one who witnessed the gates of paradise closing to the sound of music: "They close for you yet open for us." For as Ibn al-'Arabi said, music is by intention.

Actually, the Prophet ﷺ himself taught: "Actions are by intentions". While we often question the actions of the musician, what about those who listen, or more importantly, those who refuse to listen?

Once, when Rabi'a al-'Adawiyya passed by people cursing *dunyā* (the physical world), she remarked: "Had it not occupied your hearts, you would not have wasted your time cursing it!"

Similarly, if the only thing someone hears when they face the music is evil and darkness, then perhaps as Jesus said: "Every pot overflows with what it contains."

And if, as Hazrat Inayat Khan said, music is the presence immediately beneath the Divine Essence, beneath which is fragrance, is it not that the darkness one feels from sound a mirror reflecting their opinion of God?

"I am at My Servant's opinion of Me. So, let them think well of Me." Your opinion of music is ultimately what you think of Divine Communication.

You might forget how to sing, but if you hate it, you have altogether forgotten yourself.

26

Returning to the story of musical instruments as an embodiment of *sulūk*, what is the ultimate destiny of perfected *sulūk* save that one becomes a guide for others?

Yes, the musical instrument is the musician's silent *murshid* (guide). It speaks with the tongue of sacred sound: "Be like me!" It does this in the most eloquent vernacular, that of state.

The Sufis say: "The tongue of one's state is more eloquent than that of speech." Such is also the musical instrument, it teaches neither by saying or doing, but by simply being nothing.

Matisse once disagreed with his student, for the latter believed an artist can portray an object however they wish, whereas Matisse believed that an artist should observe until a vision appears.

Then, Matisse told his student that Cezanne believed every beginning artist needs to go to the Louvre to find the spirit of their guide in the paintings.

A musical instrument teaches even more with less. It breathes sound with agonizing selflessness, praying that the student-musician will listen, lessen and pay attention.

Perhaps this is what it means to not only listen attentively to one's music, but also to have *insāt* (stillness) to the inner scripture that is unfolding through sacred sound.

27

Continuing with the guidance of musical instruments, it occurred to me years ago that the only time I can remain completely silent is when I play the piano or oud.

Even when I am singing, I am following the guidance of my instrument. The conversation is between my fingers and the strings, I do not need to be involved.

Perhaps this is the beginning of the journey of *sulūk* through music, as my instrument asks me: "Can you learn how to be completely silent? In thoughts, ideas and propositions?"

Ultimately, one's passion is whatever can keep us silent for hours, since it is only one's passion that can fulfill Imam Ali's advice: "Die before you die."

The Prophet ﷺ instructed that one's opinion of God should be hopeful at the throes of death. And so, it is only the beauty of a beatific vision that can lull us into a musical slumber.

My guide, the oud, can also tell if I am being honest. I can be silent outwardly, but my inner static will possess my fingers or, even worse, feed on the emotions meant for the strings.

My oud cherishes honesty. I can bring a mountain of emotions to music, and my instrument will help me carry it. But it will not revere any attempt to dictate the way in which this unfolds.

28

Imam Ali heard a secret from the Prophet ﷺ which he could not contain within his chest, and so he uttered it into a well that overflowed into a reedbed and the lamentation of the flute was born.

The warrior who carried the gate from the fortress of Khaybar with a single arm was overwhelmed by sound. That is a sign of his superior rank, that he could even embrace the prophetic sound for a moment.

It is related that Bayazid al-Bistami asked for a needle head opening into the prophetic station, whence he almost burnt entirely: "My Lord please close it," he cried out.

The secret passed to Ali's ear as a whisper, transmuted into the ripples of water, then was reborn once again as music. Could any medium carry the Prophet's ﷺ whispers to Ali, other than sound?

But then, what was the reed-flute lamenting exactly? The separation of the whispers from the Prophet's blessed lips? Its departure from Ali's chest, or the apparent exile of the reed from the reedbed?

Ibn al-'Arabi tells us that the word *sadr* (chest) is related to *sudūr* (ushering forth), since our chests are the storehouses of creative expression that depart from us to the world.

Perhaps, then, the reed-flute is lamenting estrangement amidst languages that cannot encompass what it wants to say, only sound.

29

Rumi sang: "The only music that is forbidden are the sounds of spoons and forks heard by the hungry." But what about those who deprive hearts thirsty for music of their sustenance?

Art, and music specifically, is justice for the oppressed and specifically those for whom there are no advocates, much like the infant who's rhetorically asked by God, on the Day of Judgment, for what crime was she killed.

As we said, music guides through sundering silence and also confronts injustice with a blunt force. It pays no attention to borders, bureaucracies or armies.

If our arms, tongues and legs will testify for or against us, then so will the sounds of spoons and knives speak of the injustices against the hungry.

However, as Mawlana Rumi hinted, the sounds of spoons, forks and knives of the rich are themselves the testimonies in the Divine Court. Let us not forget that sound and music are the primordial language.

The musician seeks not only to satiate the hungry with their art, but to enliven the dead hearts longing for one breath of sacred sound, and by doing so they resurrect all of humanity.

As the Prophet showed, birds who sing are models of faith: "They awaken with empty yet sleep with satiated stomachs."

30

The saint al-Nabulusi pointed at all the musical instruments hanging on the walls of his Sufi lodge, whence they began to make *dhikr* (remembrance) of God.

We call this a miracle, which al-Ghazali defines as *kharq al-'āda* (breaking of the habit). But perhaps all that al-Nabulusi did is reveal what musical instruments already do: remember God.

It might be a bit more subtle than that. The angry religious scholar who scolded al-Nabulusi received this miracle in response. The latter simply allowed the former to recollect what he had misplaced and forgotten: the language of the spiritual realm.

Didn't God say: "There is naught a thing save that it glorifies His Praise, but you do not comprehend their glorifications"? And are musical instruments not things?

What the angry religious scholar recollected is what he had forgotten: the above Quranic verse, the language of the spiritual realm and his own self.

More importantly, the instruments responded to the finger of a saint, otherwise known as a 'musician of souls'. Al-Nabulusi is a translator, he rendered the obfuscated remembrance of his instruments into legible Arabic.

A musician's hand is all that is needed to hear the praise of all things.

31

The Quran is married to melody, as the Prophet ﷺ emphasized in multiple statements. However, the same is true for *dhikr* (remembrance).

Afterall, the Quran is described as *dhikr* in its own verses. And whereas melody excavates emotion from scriptural verses, it heightens our ability to remember in remembrance.

In this way, music straddles both revelation and memory, for it is a journey of both emotional and memory intelligence. The psychologist might ask: "What do you remember?" but music asks: "What do your memories feel, smell and taste like?"

We return again to fragrance that is inseparable from sacred sound. If all music is born out of that primordial breath *Kun*, then doubtlessly all the notes of our past are like a pearled necklace.

Moses asked God for Aaron in order that they: "Remember You abundantly" (20:33). In response, God recounted to Moses his entire life, his memories. In other words, remembrance is there to help you make peace with your past.

And this is why remembrance must be married to melody and music: we need to dress our suffering in beauty in order to perceive the redemption within, just as God enveloped Moses' fear in-between "I cast upon you a love from Me" and "you are molded under My Gaze."

32

Muslim scholars taught music theory, musical practice and held concerts in Mecca and Medina as part of their scholarship. Music was not frivolous entertainment in their eyes, but sacred worship.

What has been lost? The ability to see with both eyes: body and spirit, which is the bane of the anti-Christ, as the Prophet ﷺ stated, that the *dajjāl* (anti-Christ) is one-eyed, whereas God is not *a'war* (one-eyed).

Mawlana Rumi said: "Beyond belief and unbelief there is a field, I will meet you there." Therein lies art and all of music, beyond "where is the proof?" or all the binary and digital perceptions of reality.

Both music and spirituality are the bane of modern religious education, because they are matters of taste, and taste cannot be a curriculum.

My guide, Shaykh Hisham Kabbani said that "spirituality is all art and art is all spirituality. You need good *dhawq* [taste] to belong to a spiritual path and enjoy good art."

Those obsessed with reality being either *halal* (allowed) or *haram* (forbidden) are also the ones who can neither appreciate a good song nor understand what is being said in the silence between the notes.

How can they, when they have never stepped onto the field beyond belief and unbelief?

33

Wahhabism sought to destroy shrines and musical instruments alike. It perceived both, the spirit of sound and sound of spirit, as equal threats.

Shrines remind of the unseen, while music is its tongue and language. By destroying both, religious extremists reveal they are allergic to the unseen and all things spiritual.

They are afraid of death, as God describes them, "each of them wishes they could live a thousand years" (2:96). But that is only because they think death is the end of all things. Indeed, they are atheists in a religious garb.

Had they listened to music, they would have known that the tongue of spiritual beings and the unseen is nothing but art. Angels speak music and see abstract paintings.

As Gandalf told Pippin when the latter exclaimed: "I did not think it would end this way", he replied: "End, no, the journey doesn't end here. Death is just another path, one that we all must take. The grey rain-curtain of this world rolls back, and all turns to silver glass, and then you see it. White shores, and beyond, a far green country under a swift sunrise."

Indeed, it is amazing that a fictional character can understand reality better than custodians of religion, but such is the irony of art.

34

The spark of the Golden Age of Arabic music was a breath from Quran reciters like Uthman al-Mawsili to Sayyid Darwish. But he did not teach him Quran, rather songs and melodies.

Al-Mawsili knew that the Quran is the ultimate source of musicality, just as *Kun* is the fabric of every form in existence. But sometimes scripture appears unveiled while other times it manifests behind the myriad of forms in the universe.

As Ibn al-'Arabi says to God: "You, whose Hiddenness is naught but utter manifestation." Al-Mawsili and Ibn al-'Arabi knew that 'abodes have rulings'. The time of religion married to music had ended. The shrines were destroyed and musical instruments burnt.

And when He hides His Speech behind folk songs and melodies of the masses, like Darwish's *Zuruni* or Dylan's *Tambourine Man*, then the Named becomes even more present behind these new forms.

And those who refuse to see Him behind the veil and beyond the vale simply cannot distinguish between name and Named.

These are the makers of literal translations whom Voltaire laments, "who by rendering every word weaken the meaning! It is indeed by doing so that we can say that the letter kills, and spirit gives life."

Obi Wan knew that it was not wise to go back to the Jedi Temple after the rise of the Empire.

35

Returning to sound and remembrance, in the Quran God states that "in this is a memory for the one who has a heart or cast their listening while witnessing" (50:37).

Why is the heart the foundation of listening? Because it is the only faculty capable of perceiving the stormy ocean of Divine Manifestations.

As Ibn al-'Arabi tells, the *qalb* (heart) is from *taqallub* (fluctuation), whereas the *'aql* (mind) is an *'iqāl* (leash) that binds one to rationality. The mind is for the material while the heart is for the ethereal.

And among the five senses, only listening is as expansive as the heart. We only see what is in front of us, touch what we reach out to, taste what we intend and can even refuse to inhale air and fragrance, but we cannot close our ears.

And so, memories arrive at the shore of the heart, always welcomed and never turned away by this gracious host. We must receive them with the arms of our listening.

We first process the sound of the past. The soundscape is the only port through which memories may sail into our being. Then, and only then will we be able to witness them in form.

"As We began the first creation so do We repeat it" (21:104). We originated in sound then form, and that is how we remember as well.

When Mustafa Ismail was first invited to perform in Cairo, he was anxious when he saw oudists sitting at a café outside his venue. He realized that his audience consists of *sammi''a* (professional listeners).

He also emphasizes that the audience guides his performance as a reciter. We spoke about the intentions of listeners who refuse to hear music, due to their fear of remembering the primordial sound.

Sufi guides mention that the attendees in a saint's *suhba* (spiritual gathering) can heighten or lower the intensity of his or her words. Their intentions and level of understanding guide the heavenly show.

The same is true for music. What responsibility does the audience have in participating in the performance? They might all sit in silence of material sound, but their thoughts continue to speak.

The inner speech of the audience manifests in ciphered hymns embedded within the music of the performer. The latter is but a channel and mirror that reflects back to the audience who they are.

Steven Spielberg believed that he had entered a temple the first time he walked into a movie theater. And he did! For the movie theater is the temple of his sacred craft.

The musician plays for the audience, and they raise their hearts to heaven with their response. The question and response in this conversation is the great homily to our relationship with God.

37

Mustafa Ismail is known as *amīr al-naghamāt* (prince of melodies), because he never recited the same verse twice the same, even when he often recited it in the same *maqām*.

This is how melody pays homage to the expansiveness of Divine Creativity. "Every day, He is in a new affair" (55:29), and as Ibn al-'Arabi describes, the Muhammadan Light ﷺ "does not manifest once to two people nor twice the same to one person."

The universe is always in a new creation, necessarily. God's knowledge is infinite and thus, as Ibn al-'Arabi says, there can be no repetition in creation.

And Divine Speech, inseparable from His Knowledge, must also contain infinite meanings. So how do these infinite meanings make themselves known in a speech that has been married to melody?

The melody cannot be the same "once to two people nor twice the same to one person." The ocean of emotions must embrace the passage of moments and time, just as *maqāmāt* heal illnesses at specific blinks of day and night, as al-Farabi states.

Each *maqām* is a galaxy, and the way these itineraries dance on the stage of the Quran is a performance of interlocking universes. Infinitude manifests in an endless and incessant procession of sacred sound. Ours is a soundscape that is a *bricolage* consisting of a few notes. Abundance from humble beginnings.

Umm Kulthum used to consult Mustafa Ismail on her songs, as he mentioned in an interview. Specifically, she invited him to her studio to listen to one phrase: "What do you think about this crescendo?"

The celebrated reciter responds: "If it were up to me, I would do it like this." She exclaimed: "You are a *dahiya* [unbelievable]! Those were my thoughts exactly!"

The prodigy Egyptian violinist 'Abduh Dagher said in an interview that anyone who wants to understand *maqāmāt* well, they need to begin from and with Quran recitation.

What does Quran recitation gift melody? The Prophet ﷺ had married the two, as we have seen. And perhaps, through this marriage, melody received the divine spark.

Rather, perhaps the Prophet ﷺ married the two to sacralize melody and music, for the two were like the Prophet ﷺ himself and his companion Abu Bakr in the cave, whence "God cast down His Tranquility upon him and aided him with unseen forces" (9:40).

Like Abu Bakr in the Prophet's presence, melody is honored to embrace Divine Speech. But it had been elected primordially since the days of *Kun*, to be the means through which true remembrance can happen. And so, the dance of sound, melody, is the only performance that can do Divine Speech justice.

39

In one of his recordings, Mustafa Ismail embodied the meanings of the Quran through melody, pitch and *maqām*. The Egyptian composer who analyzed the recitation, 'Ammar al-Shiree'i exclaimed: "If this guy is not a musician, then we musicians have no business being in the room."

He dressed the broken supplication of prophet Noah in *maqām sabā*, a fitting garment for heart-wrenching sadness. But he also did more. He relied on the first octave of the *maqām*, the *qarār* (base), to send the prophet's prayer from earth upward.

Then, the Divine Reply comes from the second octave, the *jawāb* (response). Ismail further embodied the dance of the cascading waters of Noah's flood in melodic sentences that fall down the scale, as if they are ripples slowly sliding down the mountains of sound.

He repeats the entire performance. This time he keeps the supplication in *maqām sabā* but dresses the divine response, still descending from the musical *jawāb*, in *maqām 'ajam*, the joyous yang to *sabā*'s somber yin.

Even if you do not understand Arabic or the context of the verses at hand, you should understand this musical performance with a waking heart. This is why melody is inseparable from the Quran, so that it can translate Divine Speech into the universal language of hearts, not minds.

During a conversation with one of Mustafa Ismail's students and renowned Quran reciter Ahmad No'aina' he said that Ismail could not recite Quran until he had eaten to his fill, almost out of breath and with a cup of tea next to him.

No'aina' mentioned this while emphasizing that he himself could never eat before reciting at a gathering. Thus, Mustafa Ismail emerges as a unique miracle in this regard.

But why must he satiate the body before reciting Quran? Is it a matter of having enough energy to expend sprinting across the hills and mountains of soundscape, of *maqāmāt*? Or is it perhaps to balance the nourishment of body and spirit together?

But what is the satiation of the spirit in this case? Well of course, Divine Speech dressed in *maqāmāt*. Mustafa Ismail ascended with each verse in a *mi'rāj* (curved climb) across both, the universe of the octave and meanings of the Quran.

The *maqāmāt* (stations) of Mustafa Ismail satiate not only as a golden plate presented to Divine Speech, but also in how they translate God's Words to our own memories through emotions, which is the alphabet of music.

If one does not witness every breath in the *kitāb mastūr* (lined scripture) as a birth in the *kitāb marqūm* (ciphered scripture, the human being), the listening act is neither complete nor perfect.

41

In his celebrated musical rendition of Ahmad Shawqy's *Mudnak* (Your Love's Suffering), *mūsīqār al-ajyāl* (the musician of generations) Muhammad 'Abd al-Wahab dressed his teacher's words in the garment of *hijāz*, whence the large interval between the notes that is emblematic of this *maqām* aptly embodied love's separation.

Then, he does the unexpected: he makes one word in each of the first few verses stand outside the melodic space and time, as he climbs beyond the inflection point and renders them in the branching *rast* resting above the root *hijāz*.

It is both a ruse and foretelling of what is to come. A word dressed in *rast* signals a possible hope of triumph in the face of this pain of separation in love but quickly dissipates as the singer returns back to *hijāz*.

But then, 'Abd al-Wahab fully switches into this branching *rast* in the middle of the song, where the lover gains strength and courage to admonish the beloved: "Your eyes betray my pure blood, will your cheeks be treacherous as well?"

But then, the inevitable happens. The beloved and love itself conspire against the lover: "My soul is in his hand. He lost it, may his hand be blessed … as my chest is his temple!"

'Abd al-Wahab's story of *maqām* enliven Shawqy's words. It is as Ibn al-'Arabi describes, when the speaker's breath grants life to speech.

42

I wonder about the myriad of emotions I feel when I listen to 'Abd al-Wahab's *al-Nahr al-Khalid* (The Immortal River). The intense barrage of feelings, I am certain, is a result of the fact that I had heard this song during my childhood, in more innocent times.

'Abd al-Wahab's phrases are simple and predictable. It is an easy medicine. As I take in each of the main expressions in *maqām kurd*, I find myself strolling in memories, across white courtyards of marble from my childhood.

I am in Baghdad before the First Gulf War, before diaspora and exile. I let myself go in-between the oud's strings and the composer's intentions. Will you finally grant me closure, oh 'Abd al-Wahab, in this immortal river of yours?

But all music is question and answer, an octave of *qarār* (base) and another of *jawāb* (response). The former builds up tension and the latter alleviates it. As Ibn al-'Arabi describes, creation takes place between a twin dance of a *nafas nafīs* (precious breath) and a movement of *tanfīs* (alleviation).

Likewise, 'Abd al-Wahab provides melodic closure. I replay and revisit the war and migration in his words of sound. The bombs are still there in memory, the death and separation is still there. But at least the sounds of the oud can triumph over the noise of missiles and screams of the innocent, if only for a few moments.

43

The Egyptian composer Hani Shnouda emphasizes that "music is a language. It has all the components of a tongue. Subjects, objects, verbs, prepositions, questions and answers."

He then demonstrates with Mozart's Symphony No. 40, which was adopted by the inimitable Fayruz in her song *Ya Ana* (Either Me). Shnouda states that Mozart had musically presented a conversation between two people.

This is what we find also in 'Abd al-Wahab's miraculous introduction to Umm Kulthum's *Inta 'Umry* (You are My Life), a musical conversation between the Qanun and Bass consisting of only a few notes, sometimes as few as one.

But how does the ancestral music speak differently than its child, our everyday speech? What makes the *qarār* and *jawāb* more eloquent than a question mark and period?

Because there are no wasted syllables in music. Rather, there are no misplaced breaths. Music is a collective effort, not only between musician and audience, but also between all the notes of a *maqām*.

Even if a wrong or out of tune tone were to be played, it is embraced by the deluge of sound, like an unintended brushstroke that becomes part of the dance on canvas.

Such is art, it is generous!

More on wrong notes! Miles Davis famously said: "There are no wrong notes. It is always the note after that makes it right or wrong." Is it possible to have a perfect intonation on a fretless instrument like the oud?

I was amazed when I learned that Farid al-Atrash almost always played off-tune. But what is off tune when *maqāmāt*, as Simon Shaheen and Shereef Hussein emphasize, are nothing but intervals.

As we discussed, the degree of *rast* was never exactly C4. It was always either slightly lower or higher depending on the musician's style, not to mention it was rarely, if ever, according to 440Hz tuning.

I can play *jins hijāz kār* on the oud beginning from any note and it would still be correct. While commenting on the Quranic verse: "They are *fī labs* [confused] about a new creation" (50:15), Ibn al-'Arabi reads the verse as "They are *fī libās* [clothing] of a new creation".

Transpositions are attempts to accommodate a singer's voice, and 'wrong' notes are also challenges to accommodate a new character on the stage of strings and ensembles.

Perhaps, I was imprisoned by the frets of the guitar because I intuitively felt that the ability to play off tune, without frets, is the more analog and natural way of music. I learn by weaving a narrative that makes sense, not by being forbidden from writing a bad one.

45

Sometime ago, as I was listening to Farid's *taqsīm al-rabī'* (Spring) while driving, I found myself crying profusely. I had finally heard the sound behind the music.

Just as the *mu'adhdhin*'s melody in Jordan made me weep as a child, Farid's agonizing conversation with the strings of his oud opened a portal, I was able to glimpse what the music is trying to say.

I was moved even more when I saw Farid himself cry during an interview when he watched a recording of himself playing this same piece. How could he not when it was the ultimate moment of therapeutic mirroring?

But more importantly, I found myself moved less so by the words of Farid's music and more by the *ikhlās* (sincerity) in each note, the glissandos and vibratos that embraced almost every tone of his *bayātī* was speaking to me behind a subtle cipher, even more hidden than sound.

As I mentioned in the previous reflection, Farid almost always played off tune. In other words, his soundscape was a musical *kintsugi*, a series of off tune notes held together by the gold of sincere emotion.

Or as al-Sikandari exclaimed: "How much better is a sin that leaves behind humility than a good deed that leaves behind arrogance" and Beethoven: "To play a wrong note is insignificant. To play without passion is inexcusable." Music ties it all together, altogether!

I listen to Mouji's compositions, *ʿUyūn al-Qalb* (The Eyes of the Heart) and *Risāla min taḥt al-Mā* (A Letter from Beneath the Water) and I am moved to think deeply about *maqāmāt* as lenses that make meaning more vivid.

The *bayātī* in the first song embodies the heart wrenching performance of a lover in distress: "You speak and walk away, while I stay up all night and never sleep. My beloved keeps me awake, your love that is. I write upon the nights your name my beloved."

The words of ʿAbd al-Rahman al-Abnoudi come to life as they dance with Mouji's melody. These are simple musical phrases that pay homage to the poet's vernacular of and for the people.

In *Risala*, Mouji's melodies stand in awe of Nizar Qabbani's words and ʿAbd al-Halim Hafidh's voice. The composer chooses *ʿajam* to begin his journey with the audience, one that also sojourns in the death throes of love.

It is yet another ruse, since before long he modulates to *hijāz* and brings back that indomitable separation captured in the large interval of the *maqām*, and we find ourselves embraced by the words: "You have embodied life for me like a poem, then planted your wounds in my chest and took away my patience."

Musicians are miracle workers, for they change our entire perception of language, not as an end but rather a potential awaiting melody.

47

While speaking with my oud teacher Dr. Ahmad al-Khatib about the giant Riyad al-Sunbati, I told my teacher: "I can figure out what Farid or 'Abd al-Wahab are saying, but not Riyad. He is in a league of his own", to which he said: "Yes, they are great technical masters, but Riyad has a *qudsiya* [sanctity]. He is in a heaven of his own."

As I have spent the past few years solely studying Riyad's *taqāsīm* (sg. *taqsīm*, improvisation), I find myself understanding every word but unable to describe the entire narrative in fitting words. It is like Derrida's chaos of meaning that is always in *différence* and *déférence*, constantly sliding just beyond our reach.

I am also reminded by one of my friends who recounted studying a description of the Prophet ﷺ at a school in Yemen, where I later visited. He could understand every word of the *hadith*, but could not digest or taste the entire narrative, that is until our guide the saint Habib 'Umar b. Hafidh walked in, and it all made sense.

Musicians like Riyad do not compose from the first octave of reality. Rather, they witness the higher octave, of the Divine *Jawāb* (response) and then distill in ciphered phrases whatever they can capture.

Their cups runneth over and the ocean has endless waves. There is no point in lingering at each syllable. Simply trust that more is coming. And if you understand the tree, you will have tasted every fruit.

After spending years in Mustafa Ismail's and Riyad al-Sunbati's company, I concluded that Ismail is the Riyad among the Quran reciters while Riyad is the Mustafa Ismail among the composers.

Just as Ismail was – and is – *amīr al-naghamāt* (prince of melodies) who never recited a verse twice the same, even if in the same *maqām*, Riyad was always unpredictable, speaking and peeking from a peak of sanctity, as Ahmad al-Khatib mentions.

Ismail always surprised his audience like the kindergartener who drew God and when told: "Nobody knows what He looks like", he responded: "Now they do!" Similarly, Ismail made his audience think he is reciting in *sabā*. They settled down, and before long, he let them know they have been in *bastah nigār* all along (*sabā* resting on *rāhat al-arwāh*).

Likewise, when 'Abd al-Wahab and others had played it safe by composing all of Umm Kulthum's songs in *maqām kurd* or thereabouts, Riyad comes in like a storm with *rāhat al-arwāh* in *al-Atlal* (The Ruins), thereby producing what has been agreed upon by many as the greatest Arabic song of the 20th century.

If, as al-Dabbagh says, that the Arabic of the Quran has a different light than normal spoken Arabic, then Riyad's notes might also have the same sonorous form as those spoken by other musicians, but their spirit is altogether different.

49

I think about Riyad's two *taqāsīm*, the one in *hijāz* and other in *bayātī*. In the first, he modulates to the second *maqām* briefly, while in the second *taqsīm* he modulates to a relative in *shajan* (somber emotion), *maqām sabā*.

And yet, I am surprised by my reaction. I find the sojourn in *hijāz* in the first *taqsīm* with only a brief transition to *bayātī* to be much more emotionally evocative than in the second case, where the residence is in *bayātī* with only a brief migration to *sabā*.

And then I realized this is not at all surprising. In the first *taqsīm*, we are in diaspora, exiled by the large interval between the second and third degrees of the *jins*, residing at the notes *kurd* and *hijāz* respectively.

The brief reunion and return home in *bayātī*, which closes the gap between the second and third degrees, feels like an embrace between lovers who had not seen one another for what seems like an eternity.

Meanwhile, a short separation in the throes of *sabā* while remaining close to *bayt* (home) in *bayātī*'s hospitality is a much more bearable tribulation.

What drastic difference does an abode make? Meanwhile, let us not forget that F sharp is a tone with two alter egos: *hijāz* or *sabā*, depending on its custodian *maqām*. Just as Gandalf IS Saruman, as he should have been.

As I listen to Riyad's *taqsīm* in *bayātī*, I realize that the simplicity of his sentences says so much. He begins, as expected, in his *istihlāl* (preamble), by fully exploring the root of the *maqām*, *jins bayātī*.

But then, he quickly ascends to the branch *jins nihāwand* and takes me by the hand for an intense nostalgic stroll. His words bring all of my childhood to a sudden flash, eloquently embraced by the notes.

As I listen, study and practice these phrases on my oud, I am reminded of a vision I had once during a session of spiritual *murāqaba* (attentiveness) with my guide Shaykh Hisham Kabbani, when I could see him pointing at a music sheet and telling me: "Pay attention to these tones!"

These two notes were A4 and B4 flat, or *husaynī* and *'ajam*, which are the two central notes in the branching *jins nihāwand*, not only in *maqām bayātī*, but many others, including *hijāz*, *rast* and *kurd*.

Riyad continues in another phrase of *nihāwand*, further sundering my distinction between past and present. I can hear every song, film and conversation between friends dancing between his fingers.

Music can blur the line between fiction and reality or actually reveal the reality that our existence is 'fiction based on a true story'. Time shows its true self in Riyad's *taqāsīm*, where he embraces rhythm every so often. Moments appear in cycles and all our beginnings and ends can return in a blink.

51

I learn from Riyad much more than the content of his work. I ask much more than "what are you saying?" or even "why are you saying it this way?"

I am reminded by Simon Shaheen's statement, that he instructs his students to study even the way that a musician blinks. Similarly, I imagine myself sitting, holding the oud and even breathing as Riyad does when I practice his *taqāsīm*.

More than that, I often find myself speaking to him: "Listen, I cannot play your work better than you. So, you play it for me, will you?" And the spirits of these ancestors are always generous.

During my creative writing phase, I found myself doing the same when I wrote my daily poem. Sometimes, I sought the spirit of one of my muses, specifically Nizar Qabbani, Mahmoud Darwish or Khalil Gibran for inspiration, and one of them always responds.

The more I internalize this process of embodiment in music, I realize that all the words and phrases of a piece might be given their due right, but if the tonality of sound is not the same as the composer's, one will never know what they had intended.

As Beethoven said in *Immortal Beloved*, music has the power to put one in the mental state of the composer. I imagine myself living in Riyad's time, during the Golden Age of Arabic music, and try to recapture that with *ikhlās* (sincerity) and *ihsān* (perfective beauty).

52

I had two dreams that I hold dear to my heart and that continue to sustain me in my journey with music, as well as the milestone of sharing this book with you.

In the first, I found myself sitting in front of all the artistic giants from Egypt: Naguib Mahfouz, Umm Kulthum, Farid al-Atrash, 'Abd al-Wahab and Riyad al-Sunbati. I was presenting my dreams and visions to them, to which their spokesperson Mahfouz replied: "Go my son, may God grant you felicity. We are supporting you!"

In the second, I am sitting next to my muse and oud idol Riyad al-Sunbati, in his house and next to the chair where he always sat. Two cups of Arabian coffee listen to us on a table, as Riyad holds his oud and tells me in a grandfatherly voice: "Take it slow my son, one step at a time. Everything that you want will happen, just be patient."

In *A Nostalgic Remembrance*, I explore the masters of every craft as its saints who have reached the summit of prowess, whence they join the choir that sings the siren song to attract those still struggling on their trek.

If you are a musician, and you perceive with conviction that your craft is your sacred path up to this summit, you should be hearing the siren song in your dreams.

Don't be surprised when the saints of your craft, the Sunbatis and Coltranes visit to let you know: "Be patient" and "We're with you!"

53

Two of my favorite songs by Umm Kulthum were, unsurprisingly, composed by Riyad al-Sunbati, *al-Atlal* (The Traces) and *Lissa Fakir* (Do you Still Remember?).

In the second specifically, I am bewildered by the dance between the lyrics and *maqām* choice. The first part of the song is in *'ajam*, a supposedly joyous *maqām*, mirroring the B flat major scale.

And yet, the words are anything but joyous: "Do you still think my heart will feel safe with you? Or do you think one word can bring back what has been lost? Or one gaze can make longing and kindness present?"

Suddenly, I hear a *qasida* (religious ode), also in *maqām 'ajam* and ornamenting the words of a medieval Arab poet, Abu Nuwwas: "My lord, I am not fit for paradise, nor strong enough to resist hell. So, gift me a repentance and forgive my sins."

My heart is further torn when I study the poet's life and find out that he was a drunkard. These words were written in a state of brokenness. Abu Nuwwas was so sincere in his humility that God immortalized his words, such that they are sung today by saints.

Similarly, admonishing the beloved with a frown might move the heart, but it is the broken smile of *'ajam* and the tears imprisoned in shattered eyes that impact us the most.

Maqām is the art of making words say more than they themselves believe they can.

54

In Umm Kulthum's masterpiece, *al-Atlal*, I am amazed by the way in which Riyad chose three verses with the word *habībī* (my beloved) and rendered each in a different *maqām*.

In the first, the line "Where in my eyes is my beloved, magically beautiful, within whom is exaltedness, majesty and bashfulness" which Riyad dresses in *rast*, emphasizing the regality and majesty of the beloved.

Then, in the second, the line "A beloved whose nest I once visited, like a lovebird that sings my pain" is eloquently given life by *maqām sabā*, making vivid the somber throes of separation between lover and beloved.

The third line, towards the end of the song: "My beloved, everything is according to a Divine Decree", which Riyad renders in *maqām hijāz*, breathes life to the inevitability of separation between lover and beloved, embodied by the large interval between the *maqām*'s second and third degrees.

Riyad makes a stunning point behind the curtain of these masterful renditions: the love between lover and beloved goes through *mawātin* (abodes), each deserving its own ruling, emotion and *maqām* (station).

The form is one and the same, for the word *habīb* is there in all three verses, but each one has its distinct season. Some are a "winter of our discontent" while another is "made glorious summer."

55

Sabā has an uncanny power to rend the heart. I remember the first time I was exposed to this *maqām*'s power, whilst listening to Muhammad Siddiq al-Minshawi's recitation of chapter 20 from the Quran, *Taha*, recounting the content words of Pharaoh's magicians.

They tell Pharaoh after they declare their faith in God and the former threatens their demise: "We will not prefer you over what has come to us of clear signs. We swear by the One who created us. Thus, do what you have decreed, for you merely end this material life" (20:72).

Al-Minshawi renders these words in a *sabā* made more somber by the unique *shajan* (heartbrokenness) in his voice. I find the magicians' total submission and sincere repentance embodied and breathing through the melody.

And Umm Kulthum's *Huwa Sahih* (Is it true?) also pays homage to this *maqām*, as she breathes life into the poet Zakariya Ahmed's words: "Is it true that love overwhelms? And departure, as they said, is misery and pain whence one day can feel like a year!"

As I write this, I am pleased to see that this song pays homage also to the Quranic verse above, where the magicians' love for God overwhelms them into accepting any punishment that Pharaoh wishes to enact upon them.

The late Lebanese flutist, Bassam Saba, also made the *nay* weep with his *sabā*, embodying the emotions of both this Quranic verse and Umm Kulthum's song in a pure anguish of sound.

It is an unwritten rule among Arabs that one listens to Fayruz in the morning and Umm Kulthum at night. Perhaps because the latter's monthly concerts were always held in the evening.

But in reality, both Fayruz and Umm Kulthum decorated the transitory moments of our lives, for the former blessed our migration from night to day while the latter from day to night.

One of the Arabic terms for the dawn, or the *barzakhī* (liminal) time between night and day, is *sahar*, which is related to *sihr* (magic), for the liminal space is always enchanting, as T.S. Eliot describes: "The intersection of timeless with time is an occupation for the saint."

Fayruz's voice comes like the nightingale that awakens you from a deep slumber. Hers is a gentle tonality that eases your arrival from the dreamland. I find myself revisiting morning at every moment in her rendition of Sayyid Darwish's *El Helwa Di*: "This beautiful girl awoke and bakes bread during the full moon, while the rooster cuckoos at dawn."

But it is *maqām nihāwand* specifically that has embraced Fayruz's voice time and again. From *Sa'altak Habibi* (I Ask You Beloved) and *Raj'een ya Hawa* (We are Returning oh Love) to Khalil Gibran's masterpiece *A'tini al-Nay wa Ghanni* (Give Me the Nay and Sing), Fayruz gave form and breath to the melancholic daze in this *maqām*.

Melody does not exist in a vacuum. It is the voice of the singer and tonality of the musician that brings it to life. A possession of beauty!

57

They say that music is a universal language, and perhaps this is most visible in the way that two singers, thousands of miles apart, give voice and melody to the same emotions.

I was mesmerized to find Fayruz's *Keefak Enta* (How Are You?) reborn in Adele's *Someone Like You*. The former sings: "How are you? They're saying you have kids now. By God, I thought you were out of the country. What do I care about the country, God bless the kids. How are you now?"

Adele echoes: "I heard that you've settled down. That you found a girl and you're married now. I heard that your dreams came true. Guess she gave you things, I didn't give to you." Despite the different cultures and languages, love is the same.

But more importantly, it is music that is equally universal and that can give voice to this shared love. Music stands as the translator of these common feelings between us.

But this overlap between Fayruz and Adele reveals both icons as archetypes, just as perhaps Celine Dion and Majda al-Roumi also stand as mirrors of the same voice that is needed by a people and nation.

When we find that Arabs need Fayruz and Majda al-Roumi as much as Americans need Adele and Celine Dion, we realize how much better the world would be if we all communicated in music instead of mind and war.

Baleegh Hamdy suffered much with love, and he poured all of this into his music. No one composed in *bayātī* like him, as can be tasted in *Ana Ba'sha'ak* (I Adore You), the lyrics for which we discussed previously.

Studying and listening to this song attentively revealed to me the degree to which a musician's dialect emerges vividly in their work. The more I listened to this song and Baleegh's *titr* (soundtrack) for the Egyptian drama *Bawwabt al-Halawani* (The Halawani Gate) the more I recognized his idioms and the way he makes emotions sound.

He often sprinkles his *bayātī* with a three-letter syllable: C4, D4, C4 (*rast, dokāh, rast*) that makes all the difference in recognizing this *maqām* as Baleegh's own and different from all others, like Riyad or Farid.

But all of these musical dialects are mere instruments in embodying the musician's emotions, the wellspring from which their music is born. And Baleegh's is a turmoil of pain.

The way in which these phrasings of sound give an emotional breath to the lyrics, which he wrote, such as: "You who conquered my soul with their love. My affair is yours, throughout life", pierces through the listener's heart.

All of this is to say that sincerity in music is when a musician pours their own pain and joy as the brick and mortar that holds together melody and word, music and world of the song.

59

This chapter would be incomplete without reflecting on Baleegh's composition for Sayyid al-Naqshbandi, *Mawlay Inni bi Babik* (My Lord, I am at Your Doorstep).

Two main points come to mind. First, Baleegh encourages us to take an important step as a society: to question and blur the line between a secular musician and sacred spiritual art.

He came to this composition with a broken heart and emerged like a 20th century version of Abu Nuwwas, whose poetry of a broken drunkard is sung now by saints across the world.

Baleegh came to the court of Divine Love with *ummiyya* (unschooledness) and an infant-like innocence. In reality, it is the same sincerity that he brought to *Ana Ba'sha'ak* which manifests again here in this religious ode.

As for the second point, it is the fact that nowadays this crucial bit of information, that Baleegh is the composer for this ode has been all but lost, or rather concealed by a religious community that feels ashamed of broken drunkards who are loved by God.

It is unfortunately not surprising that the same community who removes a chapter on *Samā'* from Qushayri's *Risala* would do the same to Baleegh from the history and narrative of this ode's birth.

Baleegh stands not only as an icon of the Golden Age of Arabic music, but also a marker of how much the Arab and Muslim world has lost since then.

'Ammar al-Shiree'i is a 'change in garb' of Egyptian music, from the large ensembles to the television station and the clothing of *titr* (soundtrack) genre.

Others like him, such as Michel al-Masri and more recently Yasir 'Abd al-Rahman and Yousif 'Abbas, grow the family of a musical production from just composer and singer, as was the case during Umm Kulthum's era, to also include the poet.

But it is al-Shiree'i's uncanny ability to make music speak, in the absence of words, that makes him truly stand apart from others in his class. This is facilitated by what other Arab musicians describe as a *rīsha naẓīfa*, or the pure sound he is able to produce from his pick.

In *Ra'fat al-Haggan*, a celebrated political drama, al-Shiree'i makes the traditional sound of the oud dance with the suspense of espionage, in an almost war-like march of sound and pomp.

In this ability, of *taswīr* (giving form and imagery) to music, al-Shiree'i stands as Egypt's own Beethoven, with whom he shares the loss of one sense, sight and hearing respectively, compensated by heightened musicality.

Al-Shiree'i was given the choice to have a surgery to fix his eyesight, but he refused, explaining that both his imagination of the world and music would be shattered.

Remarkably, we find ourselves closing our eyes when we listen to his work, perhaps to experience it as he did.

61

I cannot depart from the Golden Age without mentioning the *'andalīb* (nightingale) 'Abd al-Halim Hafidh. Coming towards the end of Umm Kulthum's generation yet passing at a young age due to liver cirrhosis, his voice stands in a galaxy of its own, much like Fayruz and Umm Kulthum.

But 'Abd al-Halim's voice feels as though it is coming from afar, at the other end of a distant tunnel. In *'Ala Hisb Widad Galbi* (Compromising my Heart's Love), one can feel the singer's greetings depart as he serenades us: "I will tell my beloved goodbye!"

'Abd al-Halim's suffering mirrored Baleegh's, hence perhaps why they both were destined to work together on my songs. The latter's painful melodies harmonized with the former's anguished voice.

As one listens to Halim's works, or any giant from the Golden Age, we are bewildered by the simplicity of the words, sincerity of melody and their lasting impact on hearts, even today.

This contrasts with the incoherence of lyrics and unconscious weaving of sound in much of today's product. More importantly, one could not often distinguish between the secular songs of Halim or Umm Kulthum and the religious odes of Sayyid Naqshbandi, for example.

The image of the human beloved as a mirror of the Divine Beloved, as Ibn al-'Arabi emphasizes, was embodied in innocent lyrics that stand right in that liminal space of the reflection.

62

My first oud teacher, Tariq al-Jundi, taught me many lessons vicariously. The first is a silent one, embodied by both his speed and *rīsha īqā'iyya* (rhythmic pick).

It is commonly understood among oud musicians that this 'king of the Arabic music ensemble' is a percussive instrument. The oud does not produce sustained sound like the violin or cello, but rather relies on plucks and *firdāsh*, or tremolo to approximate this.

Tariq's ability is to bring out the inherent possibilities of rhythm in any given note. He answers the question: "How many different ways can someone play a quarter, half or whole note?"

How does the emotion of a quarter note change when it is played as *ta, ta ti, ta ti fi* or *ta fa ti*? Alongside the answers to these questions is the important fact that Tariq shows how much the inner rhythm of words and phrases in music gives life to the piece.

Rhythm is not just an ominous time signature standing next to the clef and organizing the moments of a composition. On the contrary, it is more importantly the inner heartbeat of every word and letter of the work.

This is more pronounced in Arabic music which, as we mentioned previously, prizes itself on improvisation. For if two notes were played with the same inner rhythm, the listener cannot help but exclaim: "You have said this already!" Tariq al-Jundi makes sure his audience is always surprised.

63

Recounting his audition at the conservatory in Jordan, Tariq al-Jundi states that he played a *capris*, a particularly fast piece for his performance. Given that such a composition requires years to master, he was proud to perform this at such an early stage in his career as a musician.

The maestro who listened to his audition, who would later become his teacher, was an old man with frail joints. He listened to Tariq perform the *capris* flawlessly, after which he asked him a question that the young musician described as "destroying everything he had believed at the time."

The maestro said: "Tariq, some people you want to watch them play, while others you want to hear them play. Which one do you want to be? When you are 60- or 70-year-old like me with arthritis in your joints, do you think you will be able to play this quickly?"

Then, the maestro took the oud and played a slow piece laden with emotion that made Tariq cry. I realized when I heard this story that every musician goes through the proverbial teenage years of their craft, where they equate speed with eloquence and quantity with quality.

In reality, it is not about playing at 200bpm or 78bpm, it is about the central question: "What are you trying to say?" A sprinter has a story to tell as much as an old man contemplating the past at sunset.

Music needs – and can – embody both with precise emotion.

64

Tariq al-Jundi tells students of the oud: "Knowing the grammar of a language does not make one a poet. Similarly, knowing musical theory does not automatically make one a musician."

And yet, he also gives a hypothetical situation, where two friends want to go to Paris. One decides to enroll in French class while the other insists on immersive learning.

When the former finally arrives in Paris, he finds his friend able to speak many more words, to order coffee, hail a taxi or converse with the public. However, in a few years, the one who formally learned French will be much more capable in the language.

Al-Jundi highlights two important points. First, that just because music is an artform does not mean that its grammar, music theory, will automatically hinder a musician's expressive ability or creative flow.

Rather, the grammar of music is simply a language that allows the musician to understand what they are hearing and experiencing in terms of sound as well communicate that to the world, even if they have the musical ear.

Secondly, 'grammar' is not exclusive to spoken language or writing. Rather, it is a principle that embodies the basic building blocks of any artform, including the structure of sound, dye or brick and mortar of architecture. And yet, it is as Picasso said: "Learn the rules like an amateur, then break them like a pro."

65

My oud teacher Omar Abbad tells me that when he was still learning the instrument he would ask his teachers about the 'grammar' of a particular phrase they played, to which they would respond: "There is no way to explain it, you just have to naturally do it with progress."

I am in total agreement with my teacher in his opinion that "such an approach just does not work". One can indeed learn all the various *zakhārif* (ornaments) and sentences through which they may express themselves and improvise.

I received the same opinion from Simon Shaheen who told me that indeed *taqāsīm* can be taught, by learning the various phrases and words, in order to build a beginning musician's vocabulary.

We sometimes forget that music is a language, as Hani Shnouda emphasizes. And just as we learn in any beginning language course how to form basic sentences, by mixing and matching various subjects, verbs and objects while making sure the case endings are correct, the same applies to music.

Vocabulary for each of the three stages of a *taqsīm* can be memorized and learned slowly and gradually. Then, as a beginner I can build my confidence by forming basic sentences and conversing internally with the music I hear, proposing alternative endings and different dialects.

The Egyptians put it simply and eloquently: "*Qūl hāga*", just say something with sound!

Omar Abbad often tells me that the notes on sheet music are just a guideline, as a musician you still have to put your own *iḥsās* (feelings) into the notes.

I reflect on the contrast between this flexibility and freedom in interpreting sheet music in Arabic verses classical western music, where all the *zakhārif* (ornaments) are already given and the musician has a very small canvas to play with and add their own touch.

On the other hand, in Arabic music, a half note can be played in at least three to four ways, by breaking it into two quarter notes, tremolo, exchanging one of the quarter notes into a drone one octave lower and many other variations.

Thenceforth, not only does every rendition of a particular composition reflect the style of the musician but each different iteration that one musician plays of a piece uniquely refracts their emotional state at the time.

It is as Ibn al-ʿArabi says, Divine Manifestations do not appear once to two people nor twice the same to one person. The improvisational spirit of Arabic music, not only in *taqāsīm* but also in written compositions is a musical interpretation of the Quranic verse: "Every day He is in a new affair" (55:29).

The Prophet ﷺ says that the angels who circumambulate God's House in the seventh heaven never return again. Likewise, the sacred sounds of the heavenly orbits never repeat themselves.

67

Omar Abbad graciously told me, after studying the oud with him intensely for six months, that I need to venture on my own and learn how to practice and master a piece by myself.

Perhaps the most important lesson a teacher can give their student is to learn how to learn, to digest the process not only the content. A teacher who insists that their students continue to rely on their tutelage is perhaps unsure of their own abilities as a musician.

Let us repeat that music is a language, and the purpose of learning any language is to "know how to speak". And as Tariq al-Jundi explained eloquently, we each speak like robots when first learning a language, despite the fact that our grammar might be correct.

Indeed, two people who have perfect grammar in music reveal their varying levels of mastery through their *iḥsās* (feeling) and *balāgha* (eloquence).

Past those proverbial teenage years of a musician's growth in their craft, when they believe that quantity is quality and speed is eloquence awaits the shore of simple elegance in expression.

As Charles Bukowski states: "An intellectual makes what is simple difficult while the artist makes what is difficult easy." Bruce Lee also said: "I am more worried about the fighter who has practiced one punch 1000 times than the one who practiced 1000 moves once."

Maturity in music is patience in growth with sound by yourself and packing as much meaning into a single note as possible.

Another teacher of mine, Dr. Ahmad al-Khatib is an oud whisperer. Although I never met him in person, I vicariously learned from him how to make the strings of my instrument fall in love more deeply with my fingers.

Dr. Al-Khatib is one of three maestros from whom I learned this way, the other two being Shereef Hussein and Riyad al-Sunbati. And how fitting is it that Ahmad is the one who let me in on the secret as to what makes al-Sunbati so special: he has a particular *qudsiya* (holiness).

It was an epiphany watching Dr. Al-Khatib pluck the drone string on his oud, not with the *rīsha* (pick) as is common, but rather using all his fingers at once, a gentle flick that tells the drone: "You are free to dance as you wish."

I also pay attention to the way in which his left-hand cups the bridge of the oud in a soft embrace, and my body immediately tells me: "This is how it is supposed to be done."

Ahmad al-Khatib is indeed a unique force of musical nature. Only a virtuoso like him could compose a four-part rhapsody in *maqām sūznāk*.

And as I watch him perform, the Quranic verse: "Their hands testify" (24:24) becomes a reality for me. I realize that my hand is having a conversation with his, and I do not need to – nor should – be involved in anyway.

69

I once asked Dr. Al-Khatib: "I notice that you often keep your eyes closed while playing the oud, why?" He replied: "One of my teachers used to tell me: 'Imagine yourself while playing that you are mute and blind, and music is the only language you have to communicate with the universe.'"

It is as the Quranic verse states: "Indeed, in this is a memory for the one who has a heart or cast their hearing while witnessing" (50:37). The musician casts all their senses at the altar of sacred sound in order to be fully present, in *fanā'* (annihilation), with the primordial Creative Command *Kun!*

Even the sense of hearing, as the verse shows, should be cast. Thenceforth, the Divine Response will come: "I become the hearing with which they hear." Only then can one hear the music as it is here and now.

What is to be gained when one loses themselves entirely in the act of speaking and listening to sacred sound? The Divine Voice explains: "Whoever loves Me, I love them. Whomever I love, I kill. Whomever I kill, I become their ransom."

The only compensation for relinquishing one's entire being in the ocean of sound is as the drop that returns to the sea, becoming water itself.

Once the musician learns from their instrument how to be nothing, they become the very channel through which God Speaks.

70

Another question I asked Dr. Al-Khatib: "I can hear every single note you are playing. Even if you play very quickly, your pick has a surgical precision. How did you manage that?"

He told me: "My father was a poet who once asked me: 'Ahmad, do you know what eloquence is?' It is to say what you intend with as few words as possible such that there can be no doubt in the mind of the listener as to what you mean."

Eloquence, *balāgha* is related to *tablīgh*, or conveying a message. The more I dive deeper into the ocean of *maqāmāt* of which Simon Shaheen says we have only scratched the surface, the more I realize that eloquence, in any medium, is to make the words and phrases of the language say more than is presumed possible.

There is always an element of surprise in what a musician says through their instrument, especially in Arabic music and the art of *maqāmāt*. In the case of Ahmad al-Khatib, it is always his astounding ability to say so much with so little.

Pay attention to how early learners of a language speak: loud, sudden and with discrete words that do not seem to connect to one another naturally.

And then, a poet comes who sometimes need only to motion with their hand in order for the *tablīgh* to occur. In the case of Ahmad al-Khatib, I can often hear his music before he even starts to play. Such is *hudūr* (presence) for the artist: to perform in silence.

71

I still remember the first time I saw Simon Shaheen perform in person, at a church in Kalamazoo, Michigan in 2018. With oud and violin in hand, I witnessed something I had not anticipated.

When I met Simon during the intermission, he stood in front of me with a suit that reminisced of those worn by al-Sunbati, Farid or al-Qasabji.

Suddenly, I could hear not only his music embodied in presence and ancient thick Palestinian accent from Tarshiha, but I felt as though I am standing among all the giants of the Golden Age of Arabic music. They are all present and perform with him, while he carries their heritage upon his shoulders.

It was from this day foreword that I learned what a beginning musician should know from their teacher: not only how to play a particular piece or apply a given technique, but more importantly how to become a musical being.

This is not about speaking with a thick Palestinian accent or wearing a suit as Simon does. Rather, it is about internalizing how 'who' Simon Shaheen is participates in the music he produces.

It is as the Moroccan saint 'Abd al-'Aziz al-Dabbagh said: "Whoever knows how the Prophet ﷺ is, they will find tranquility." If we, as both al-Dabbagh and Ibn al-'Arabi state, figure out the spiritual states and breaths of a master like Simon, we can decipher the actions and words they birth in their work.

During one of the annual Arabic music retreats that Simon created, he listens to a student improvising a *taqsīm*. The latter sojourns a bit too long in the *istihlāl* (preamble) or opening stage of the *taqsīm*, at which point Simon exclaims: "You have been saying 'good morning' for 10 minutes."

As Simon also explains during the retreat: "The *taqsīm* is all about tension. You build it up then release it with questions and answers." This theme of questions and answers has been reiterated by many thus far, including Hani Shnouda and others.

And it all returns us to the important realization that music is a language, where the main objective is expression, or 'saying something' as Egyptians state simply.

If you want to repeat a phrase or word in a *taqsīm* multiple times, you should ask yourself: "What new meanings am I adding by repeating this verse? Am I changing the ornaments to emphasize different words or syllables?"

This is precisely why it is of utmost importance to learn this language from those who know how to speak it and from those like whom you want to speak as well.

I learn from Riyad all the different ways he explores a root *jins* of a *maqām*, and I begin to diversify his words as he himself would. Only then can I learn how to speak like him but in different situations and on the terrains of alternate *maqāmāt*.

73

Simon Shaheen's contribution to Arabic music in the West presents an important question: What does cultural awareness of music or a genre of music look like?

Prior to Simon's arrival in the United States, as he himself mentions, Arabic music was mostly known as a cabaret playlist. Shaheen not only founded an ensemble and produced many albums. He did something far more important.

He introduced the grammar of Arabic music as a language to be learned and understood among Western musicians and listeners. Those who have never stepped foot in the Middle East can now converse in and about *maqām*, because of Simon Shaheen.

But the question remains: what does that feel like, culturally, when a society becomes increasingly more aware and appreciative of the grammar of a musical language? At the highest level, as Ibn al-'Arabi would say, they are able to use this tongue as a means to experience and express their spirituality.

But what happens most often for the masses is the ability to process such an artform emotionally. To be able to understand what feelings are being communicated through *maqām bayātī* differently than *sabā*, *hijāz* or *nihāwand*.

That is not to say that Western listeners will sense the same nostalgia as the Arab would, for "each people know their wellspring" (2:60).

74

Stumbling upon Shereef Hussein's in-depth explanation of *maqāmāt* was a revolutionary milestone in my own understanding and appreciation of this artform.

I came to understand that being an exquisite musician and teaching music are two different things. And yet, in some rare circumstances, one finds both emotion and the ability to give voice to the ineffable together present in one teacher.

Such is Shereef Hussein, who plays the greatest hits from the Golden Age of Arabic music with as much ease as any Egyptian would drink a cup of tea after a long day at work. He is an Egyptian at heart and brings the entire legacy of his native abode and mine into his passion to teach *maqāmāt*.

As I mentioned previously, Shereef Hussein is one of a few teachers from whom I learned vicariously, by watching him play whence my hand communicated with his without my knowledge.

As I watch him play al-Mouji's and 'Abd al-Halim's masterpiece *Letter from Beneath the Water*, my fingers intuitively know how to do *firdāsh* (tremolo) peacefully. Not too fast or harsh, but like a stroll down the hill.

As the Sufis say: "The tongue of one's spiritual state is more eloquent than the tongue of speech", and this is how Shereef Hussein teaches, in complete silence of mind and presence of heart.

75

One, among many, of the incredible lessons that Shereef Hussein gives me is the connection between *ab'ād* (intervals) in *maqāmāt* and the emotional effect they have.

He highlights the relationship between *jins 'ajam* with intervals (4,4,2), *jins nihāwand* (4,2,4) and *jins kurd* (2,4,4). The migration of the '2', or half tone interval from the end in *'ajam* to the middle in *nihāwand* and the beginning in *kurd* makes all the difference in the world in the emotional power of each *jins*.

This half – or two quarter – interval is hidden far behind two whole – or four quarter – intervals in *'ajam* which grants this *jins* its joyous aura as is common among major scales.

In *nihāwand*, the half interval moves to the middle, in-between the two whole intervals, which in turn brings out the melancholy character in this *jins* much more so than *'ajam*.

Lastly, in *kurd*, the listener is met immediately with the half interval which grants this *jins* the sad character that surpasses *nihāwand* and definitively *'ajam*.

And yet, as we saw in *Lissa Fakir*, it is the *siyāgha* (usage) of the *maqām* that grants it its final emotional character in a composition. In this way, Shereef Hussein's masterful explanation highlights the importance of intervals as the definitive building blocks in *maqāmāt*, much more so than their tonic starting point.

Another eye-opening listening that Shereef Hussein gives me is the intimate relationship between *maqāmāt* and the oud. Not only is the oud the 'king of the Arabic music ensemble' but also the ink and terrain upon which *maqāmāt* developed as an artform.

Hussein highlights just how much the oud is *maqām*-centric and vice versa. Consider, for example, *maqām shāhināz*, which is often played with the tonic D4 (*dokāh*) in mind. Once we transpose this to the new tonic C4, the *maqām*'s name changes to *hijāz kār*.

The reason for this is that the word *kār* in Farsi means 'work' or 'struggle', alluding to the difficulty in using the fourth finger in playing *hijāz kār* on the oud.

One finds the same allusion in the names of notes, such as *yikāh* and *dokāh*, which simply mean 'one' and 'two', respectively, since these were the first and second strings in the past when the oud only had four strings.

The grammar of a language is not divorced from the instrument used to voice it. On the contrary, often the wood and age of the tool grows alongside the eloquence of the tongue that it sings.

This is also to emphasize that any claim to love a particular genre of music requires an equal investment in the history behind the story. Is it a sign of love that you want the instrument to mirror your emotions, yet you do not wish to listen it its soliloquy?

77

I understood the reverential love between master and disciple when I saw the virtuoso and ensemble conductor Michael Ibrahim in the presence of his guide, Simon Shaheen, after a performance a few years ago.

Ibrahim could very well be a raging river on his own, while on the stage both as a musician and conductor of the National Arab American Orchestra.

However, when in the presence of his teacher Simon Shaheen he retreats into infant-like innocence. He is still learning and willing to absorb even the blinks of his teacher.

This all shows that a musician's technical ability is merely the tip of the iceberg; what lies under the ocean is much more important: the spiritual deluge that sustains their craft.

In Egypt, such reverence is described that someone 'knows their elders'. And this could be tasted so eloquently in Ibrahim's performance alongside Simon on stage. Also quoting Egyptian musical culture: "If the teacher inhales, the student exhales."

Ibrahim is not ashamed to even travel in his *taqsīm rast* along the same itinerary as Simon Shaheen. You could almost see him tracing the guide's sound steps in the sand, not only in terms of melody and *maqām*, but even tonality. This is embodiment at its highest levels, or as the Sufis would say: "Michael disappears, only Simon remains."

Among the knowledge that Dr. Tarek Abdullah has taught me, through his lessons on the Egyptian school of oud, is the subtle idea that a school of oud, whether historically, culturally or institutionally, cannot revolve around one person.

The story of music in any given culture is a narrative, each chapter of which is written by one of the giants in its history. In Egypt, this includes Darwish, 'Abd al-Wahab, Qasabji, Riyad, Umm Kulthum, Farid, Baleegh, 'Abd al-Halim and countless others.

Dr. Abdullah also highlights the importance of passion about a craft as more than just learning how to play one or two compositions. Foregoing learning the Arabic/Farsi names of degrees in a *maqām* or that *nisba sīka* is not merely a transposition of *nisba rāhat al-arwāh* might be doing more than just simplifying learning *maqāmāt*; it could be altogether distorting the artform.

As I mentioned previously, it is not a sign of true love to want to speak to the oud with your emotions yet not be willing to listen to its own history and story.

"If you are grateful I will grant you more" (14:7), and if you are willing to listen to your musical instrument's own story, beginning with recognizing that wood remains living, then you will be surprised at how much the instrument gives back to you in listening and sincerely translating your emotions to sound.

79

Despite being born in Baghdad, the Iraqi school of oud never captured my heart as much as the Egyptian school. That is not to say that I do not like Iraqi songs or musicians. On the contrary, *Foug al-Nakhal* (Above the Palm Tree) by Nazim al-Ghazali remains one of my favorites from the Golden Age.

However, in truth, I cannot explain why I like the school of Riyad, 'Abd al-Wahab, Baleegh and Umm Kulthum more than the Basheer brothers or Naseer Shamma, for this is a matter of taste. And *dhawq* (taste), as Shaykh Hisham Kabbani states, is married to spirituality.

And despite the immense effect which Shamma's *'Amiriyya* composition had on me, as I discussed during the introductory chapter, I absolutely disagree with his statement that there is no Egyptian school of oud, only individual maestros, or that the eastern school of oud is more *hirafiyya* (technical) whereas the Iraqi school is *ta'bīriyya* (expressive).

In my humble opinion, this signals a misunderstanding of the eastern school, for what is a *maqām* save an itinerary for self-expression through melody?

And one merely needs to listen to Khalid Muhammad Ali or Ali al-Imam, two prodigy students of the Bashir brothers and the Iraqi school to understand that *maqāmāt* are emotion, expression and meaning weaved into a tapestry of melody and sound.

Ibn al-'Arabi tells us that the first instance of *tarab* (musical ecstasy) is when the Divine Chair hears the differentiation of the utterance *Kun* into a command and prohibition or news about the past, present and future.

In turn, the first movement of love from God towards us is of sound speech while our first movement of love towards Him is born out of listening.

Ibn al-'Arabi's perception of the oneness of being, *wahdat al-wujūd*, entails that everything we experience in our material existence is a mirror reflection of a spiritual reality that is ultimately rooted in God.

And so, this *sawt sarmad* (primordial sound) and original experience of *tarab* is hardly an abstract concept. Rather, it is a timeless movement that continues to unfold incessantly in time.

Every instance of *tarab* that a listener feels while listening to sound, in its full spectrum as Habib 'Umar highlights, is the resurrection of an ancient memory, when all things heard the Divine Voice.

More importantly, the sounds we are drawn to, we listen to attentively. My own attraction to the oud, more than any other instrument, and the musical voice of Riyad specifically are various delineations of *ma'rifat al-nafs* (knowledge of self). God speaks to us through our *isti'dād* (disposition) as Ibn al-'Arabi states, thereby sacralizing the mundane.

81

Ibn al-'Arabi also states that music is tethered to the rotation of the heavenly orbits and Divine Realities that plant the wellspring of emotions in us.

In turn, our feelings of sadness or joy when listening to music are the result of our interaction with these Divine Realities. Although the Andalusian mystic seems to insinuate that emotional affection indicates a lesser level of *samā'*, listening to music, than receiving *ma'rifa* (gnosis) of God, here he gives more subtle explanations.

Our emotions are transparent metaphors that open a path to perceiving the Divine Reality which sustains us behind the material and psychosomatic dimensions.

It is only if I fail to contemplate the 'why' of my emotional reaction to music that these feelings of sadness, happiness or nostalgia cease to be a means for *ma'rifa* and instead become a barrier to what Ibn al-'Arabi calls *al-samā' al-mutlaq* (absolute listening).

The Andalusian mystic does not seek to belittle the emotional or material experiences of music. On the contrary, he wishes to sacralize the human experience. As Bill Moyers highlights: "Creativity is piercing the mundane to find the marvelous."

Moses found God at the burning bush, because he sought light and warmth. And He also speaks to us through those forms and sounds we are most in need of, emotionally and materially.

82

The Andalusian mystic also harmonizes between the four strings of the oud and the four humors of the human body: phlegm, blood, black and yellow bile.

This is material and immanent metaphysics at its best. Ibn al-'Arabi does not even discuss music here, only the form of the musical instrument, highlighting the sacredness of the wood that we mentioned in a previous reflection.

He is also emphasizing the similarity between the human being and musical instrument, since the former also has a vocal system that combines both wind and string channels of sound.

What emerges from all of this is the necessity to regard both, the musical instrument as a living being and musician as an instrument in the Hands of the Divine Musician.

As we mentioned beforehand, every musician's instrument is a silent guide, seeking to teach its disciple, the musician, by simply being. The mirroring is in full bloom when the human musician can be in the hands of God as their instrument is in their hands.

The reflection in the mirror will be inverted back to its original form. The Right Hand of God moves, and the musician's left hand speaks, only to return as the right hand of music in the oud, flute or cello.

Only then can one hear all of sound in the stillness of the musician.

83

Ibn al-'Arabi also exclaims that "poets extinguish their words in existent things. This one writes about women, the other about wealth, status or power. However, the knowers of God only see one behind all these forms."

There is naught a musician who has written a single verse of sound save that it is God who was sought and seeking through those breaths. It matters not the faith or even sincerity of the artist.

As Ibn al-'Arabi also mentions, "every human being with an imagination, when they imagine, then their gaze extends to the Divine Presence."

Some of these symphonies of sound produced throughout human history are easier for many of us to perceive as Divine in ultimate origin. Beethoven's *Moonlight Sonata*, Mozart's *Symphony No. 40* or Chopin's *Nocturne Op 9 No 2* translate the movements of the heavenly orbits with subtle eloquence.

And yet, I already know that Mustafa Ismail's melodies and Riyad's *taqāsīm* move me in ascension far more than even Beethoven or Chopin.

And so, why is it farfetched that even what some of us consider to be lowly music can still be married to the dispositions of some. "Every people have come to know their wellspring" (2:60). Yet, an oasis is naught but a mirage, where one "finds God there" (24:39).

In commenting on the source of inspiration for his magnum opus, the *Meccan Openings*, Ibn al-'Arabi says: "My spiritual state while composing this work is not my current condition now. Thus, you the reader might very well comprehend my words better than me, for my spiritual state then could be yours."

The Prophet ﷺ said: "The one receiving a lesson might very well understand it better than the one conveying it." All of this is only possible if one internalizes the fact that they are not the source for their breaths.

And so, Derrida's proverbial 'death of the author' emerges as a necessary selflessness in the musician who perceives themselves as a channel for God's Breaths. Put differently, as Elizabeth Gilbert mentions in her TED talk, "Your Elusive Creative Genius": "Traditionally, artists were never thought as geniuses, but they had a genius."

We return once again to the musical instrument as the ultimate guide. It is burnt, separated from home, emptied from the inside and holes are dug in its body, and yet it is not the one praised for the music, only the human musician.

What claim can an instrument make over the music it sings? And what ownership can we have over the flood of creative inspiration that passes over our banks. Even a draft of our work is but a draft of wind gifted from above.

85

Mawlana Shaykh Hisham Kabbani tells me once, during a *hadra* (ecstatic Sufi dance) at his lodge and mosque in Burton, Michigan when I explain to him that some Muslim scholars do not agree with this ritual: "Do you see all these people moving ecstatically?" he says: "If I were to not allow them to do this, they would all be outside in the world expending this energy in violent ways."

What is music if it does not move us somehow into ecstasy? "Oh, you who believe, what is the matter with you when it is said to you go in the way of God that you remain heavy and attached to the earth" (9:38).

In other words, how can you not be moved by sound? If the Divine Creative Command *Kun* moved the Divine Chair into ecstasy and continues to cause the heavenly orbits to revolve in a cosmic dance, what kind of heart does one have that is not moved by the rhythm of creation and Divine Grammar, otherwise known as music?

"Indeed, some rocks break apart whence rivers flow therefrom, while from others water gushes forth, while others fall from the majesty of God" (2:74).

Perhaps, if our hearts are like rocks then we need to listen to music more until the rivers of emotion gush forth. Wondrously, nowadays it is often the hearts of religious scholars that are not moved by music, while those who are not aware they have been speaking with Him all along are most moved by His Melodies.

The first time I ever performed the oud in public was in front of my guide Shaykh Hisham Kabbani. He closed his eyes and listened to me speaking the notes as an infant, still learning a language for the first time.

I watch his spiritual state and interpret as much as I can on the Oud. I understand at that moment that, as Beethoven said: "To play a wrong note is insignificant. To play without passion is inexcusable."

The presence of the saint in front of me speaks to me in silence: "Your ability to play well will come in time, but your willingness to be present with the music starts now."

The hundreds of people in attendance disappear. The only face and fragrance I perceive, even now in my imagination, is the guide. I realize that he was not simply listening but teaching me what I would only discover much later.

He sanctified my journey. If I had not played in front of my guide then, none of what has materialized since then would have been born. He listened, and thus everything else also heard.

"So, this is what you want to do?" And he saw and witnessed. The realization came that I process reality through sound, since the first time I heard the *adhān* in Jordan and was moved to tears. In this moment of time, all of the past and future continues to unfold therefrom, like a climax with an endless crescendo.

87

Shaykh Hisham Kabbani tells me: "If anyone wishes to move you to do something, they come to you in your dreams. Otherwise, they can tell you a thousand times in a waking state, it will not move you an inch."

The Prophet ﷺ also said: "If someone tells you that a mountain has moved from its place, you can believe them. But if they tell you that someone's disposition has suddenly changed, don't believe them."

Ibn al-ʿArabi explains that dreams take place in *ʿālam al-khayāl* (realm of imagination) where creative inspiration and Divine Revelation also descend upon the hearts of humanity.

Otherwise, what could behoove artists and musicians to push themselves to the precipice of practical self-destruction seeking to translate the ineffable into the tangible?

It is as Leonard Cohen exclaimed: "If I knew where great songs came from, I would go there more often. It is definitely a gift." It is a wonderland where miracles happen, as al-Dabbagh mentions, where even a hair can carry a mountain.

And if we agree with Hazrat Inayat Khan that sound is the primordial language, then music is sacred communication of the highest order. One would be wise to listen to what was revealed at that intersection, of timeless with time, as Eliot describes.

On my way back from giving a lecture on Jesus in Ibn al-'Arabi's writings, where I discussed the importance of the former's *bashariyya* (of flesh and blood) in the Quran and the Andalusian mystic's works, I was behooved to drive to Shaykh Hisham's Sufi lodge to attend the weekly session of *dhikr* (remembrance).

As soon as I entered the gathering, I could see the guide sitting in front on his chair. He immediately greeted me with: "Welcome Dr. Ali, *abshir!* (Await a glad tiding!)" I immediately perceived the saint's channeling of Divine Serendipity: *bashariyya* and *bishāra* are both linguistic and metaphysical relatives.

Jesus is the 'Word made flesh' and, hence, the one who is allowed to give the *bishāra* of the coming of the Prophet ﷺ in the Quran (61:6). But these connections could have arrived by reading or intellectual study of the material.

Rather, what makes this exchange important is that the saint emerges as a liminal space where creative inspiration and process are simultaneously born, the latter of which I describe in *A Nostalgic Remembrance* as "making connections where none seem possible or exist."

The Prophet ﷺ said: "If God loves someone, He grants them a caller from their own self." And every piece of music that is born in the heart of a musician is their inner saint voicing the primordial *Kun!*

89

Mawlana Shaykh Hisham Kabbani explains to me the way in which *kashf* (unveiling) occurs in the Naqshbandi Sufi path. While holding a *tasbih* (prayer beads) in his hand, he says: "Whereas in other paths, the disciple begins to perceive openings right away, just like moving across these beads from the front to the back, in our path the openings come in reverse. The last veil to be lifted is vision and the disciple discovers how much they have progressed unawares."

Unsurprisingly, I have found this to be an antidote for a musician's journey. If we are constantly pushing the boundaries of excellence with our daily practice and self-discipline, it can be difficult to gauge how much progress one has made.

Thus, it is important every once in a while, to go back and play the compositions that one found very difficult a year ago. We find that we grew immensely, and the previous veils have been lifted, but we are simply in a darker depth of the ocean than before.

This is a crucial lesson in both spirituality and creativity. As Ibn 'Ata Allah al-Sikandari explains in his *Aphorisms*: "A sign of felicity at the ends is returning to one's beginnings."

We need to find the safe spaces in our craft. For the musician, it is the simple compositions, or even not so simple yet those that we have loved so intensely into mastery, and into which we can retreat when the journey feels difficult. The trek never ends, and our fragility is perhaps the most musical expression we have.

When I heard Adele's newest song, *Easy on Me*, I found myself weeping. An epiphany opened in front of me. I no longer heard the voice of the singer, but rather myself standing in front of God on Judgment Day.

"Go easy on me! I was just a child, and didn't have the chance to choose what I chose to do. So go easy on me!" When I share this reflection in public, I am ostracized by someone because "this song is about motherhood, not God."

I am immediately reminded by the lesson which the Prophet ﷺ sought to teach his disciples, when a mother finds her lost son and embraces him tightly: "Do you think this woman would throw her child to the fire? God is more merciful with His Creation than a mother is to her child."

And Ibn al-'Arabi also tells of a man who makes claims about good deeds he never did to enter paradise. God allows him to pass, whence the angels say: "But he's lying!" To which God responds: "I know, but I do not wish to put his gray hair to shame."

As artists generally and musicians specifically, we come to sound with all our mistakes and shortcomings, to present a testimony that there is beauty nevertheless in our faults and others'. The melodies we weave are intercessions of sound, seeking God's Mercy for all. Often, we are not even sincere, but He listens anyways.

91

Fela Kuti explained it well: "Music is a spiritual thing; you don't play around with music." This is a challenge that many religious musicians face, due to the unfortunate dissonance between music and faith in many contemporary religious communities.

Some of us, unfortunately, practice their craft in spite of their faith. Others are always afraid and careful that their craft does not distract them from God. Others still have left their craft behind, neglecting the Divine Gift, thinking that this is what God wants.

In all instances, when many of us do practice or listen to music we leave the sacred behind. It is not a time when spiritual awareness is at its highest, rather the focus is on the flow and being in the moment.

But practicing music only when the flow or creative inspiration is present ignores the source and the Giver of this gift. For the musician, this craft is what Ibn al-ʿArabi calls our *wajh khāss* (intimate private direction) to God.

We enter into its presence as we do a prayer niche, leaving ourselves open to the unexpected Divine Grace. Just as Mary the mother of Jesus was in her seclusion, whence Zechariah asked her: "Where did you get this sustenance?" and she said: "It is from God who gives whomever He wills without measure" (3:37). So, let us come to our craft as our intimate prayer niche. Then, the gifts of sound will arrive at our doorstep from every unexpected direction.

92

In *What is Islam? The Importance of Being Islamic*, Shahab Ahmed describes Islam not as a system of rituals and beliefs, but rather a 'process of making meaning'.

How does this translate for crafts, the arts and music specifically? It means that every ritual and dimension of Islam can be interpreted as a stage in the creative process and weaving the tapestry of sacred sound.

Specifically, the three dimensions of Islamic spirituality, *sharī'a* (law), *tarīqa* (path of self-discipline) and *haqīqa* (spiritual reality) should manifest for the musician on the journey towards mastery.

The *sharī'a* of music is its grammar and theory, whereas the *tarīqa* is the discovery of shortcomings and weaknesses within the craft and the struggle to rectify those faults.

Lastly, the *haqīqa* of music is when the meditation on the technical contours of craft and instrument delivers the musician to the summit of mastery, where they join the choir of the siren song and begin to express universal wisdoms, using their technique as the building blocks.

Religious scholarship is but one craft and path up the mountain of sainthood, while music remains one of the most sacred treks that allows one to communicate using the primordial language of the spiritual realm.

93

In a study on the 'four stages of mastering a musical instrument', a researcher delineates steps that eloquently summarize the spiritual journey of *sulūk* (self-discipline).

The first stage is 'unconscious incompetence', which is a polite way to say that one doesn't know and doesn't know that they don't know. I reminisce watching musicians play the oud and thinking to myself: "This is not hard; I should be able to learn this instrument quickly."

The second stage is 'conscious incompetence', when the seeker begins to consciously work on rectifying their faults and weaknesses (e.g., how to hold the instrument correctly, strengthening the fourth finger, etc.).

The third stage is 'conscious competence', when the musician becomes aware of their improvements and technical growth in the craft. They schedule their practice and witness the changes in real time, but this is still not the height of mastery.

That arrives in the fourth stage, 'unconscious competence', when the musician enters a type of Nirvana or *fanā'* (annihilation), whereby music becomes a conversation between their hands and the instrument.

However, in all of this, the musician-seeker is not only rectifying their weaknesses on the instrument. Our instrument is a mirror that reflects back what stands between us and being musical beings.

I reflect on the note E4 half flat, which has been standardized as *sīkāh*. Traditionally, this note is slightly lower than E4 half flat in *maqām bayātī*, slightly higher in *rast* and higher still in *sīkāh*.

But even if one were to play the note exactly the same in all three *maqāmāt*, the emotional power of the tone changes entirely. In *bayātī*, this degree is nostalgic, while in *rast* it is majestic and jovial in *sīkāh*.

Recognizing this subtlety allows me to appreciate the relational tonality of notes. The emotional power of any particular note does not exist in a vacuum. Rather, it is entirely dependent on the note before and after.

It is as Miles Davis mentioned: "There are no wrong notes. It is the note after that makes it right or wrong." A phrase or musical sentence is a collective effort between all the notes. Just as the Prophet ﷺ described believers, as a body whose limbs rush to each other's aid when one of them is sick or wounded.

And from this *hadith* and this relationality of notes we understand that each of us is a degree in the symphony of our surroundings. We need to realize that our roles and emotional effectiveness depend entirely on our adjacent human notes.

As Sufi mystics highlight, the spiritual level and energy of those attending the *suhba* (gathering) of a saint can either heighten or lower the level of the discourse, regardless of the saint's own rank.

95

Ibn al-ʻArabi states that each person receives Divine Inspiration through one of the five senses. Some people process reality as sound, smell, touch, taste or vision.

Today, we consider it a medical condition when some people smell colors or see sounds as hues, but in reality, it is a heightened spiritual perception.

Whatever your primary sensory medium of communication, you will struggle until you acknowledge and fully embrace this path. For musicians, we process reality as sound.

I often speak with young people who tell me that they ask God questions for which they receive no response. And yet, they find themselves always at the threshold of their musical instrument.

I need only ask them: "Have you ever thought about asking Him through your music?" To which they always reply: "I never thought about it!" As musicians, we need to realize that our instrument is the burning bush.

As John Caputo says in *On Religion*: "God is not the answer, but the opening of the question." We ask Him questions seeking answers in the distance.

However, we do not realize that He is the One posing the queries through our tongue of choice.

The Egyptian oudist Mamdouh Al-Gibali says that if someone has the gift of music, it will remain there, dormant, until someone or something awakens it.

No matter which path a musician takes, that strays away from their passion, they will find themselves, sooner or later, at the threshold of sound and an instrument of choice.

As George Lucas explained, he had many different career choices: anthropology, national geographic, filmmaking but regardless of whichever path he would have taken, he would eventually make *Star Wars*.

Those of us destined for music are elected as such because God wills to reflect upon His Names and Attributes through a mirror of sound within us, one that harmonizes with our disposition, as Ibn al-'Arabi would say.

We also need to understand that creativity is energy that needs to be expended, for better or worse. A musician will either channel this force in a canvas of sound that embodies the hero's journey sonorously, or it will force itself out of us in more violent ways.

As Ernest Hemingway beautifully put it: "As a human being, I judge vices but as a writer I should not judge, I should first understand." We spill sound on track, so we do not have to spill blood in the world.

97

The art world, and music specifically, often has the reputation of being very corrupt. Many musicians do indeed commit suicide or at the very least exhibit self-destructive tendencies.

But the reason for this is not because art or music is inherently corrupt. Birds sing much more eloquently than human beings yet do not exhibit the same behavior.

It is because, as Fela Kuti stated previously, "music is a spiritual thing, and you don't play around with music." The artist endangers their own self when they don't acknowledge their craft as sacred worship.

For the musician specifically, our craft is communicating in the tongue of the spiritual realm. We must recognize the energy fields we are stepping into through the plucks of our instrument.

This is why an immanent and intimate spirituality is crucial for the artist, one that does not juxtapose their craft in opposition to God but rather in apposition.

As al-Dabbagh states, the *fath* (spiritual opening) is like a mountain that falls on a hair; and with Divine Authority, the hair can indeed carry the mountain.

We seek God as musicians and artists in order to appreciate the gift and fully understand what is being said in the unsaid of silence.

The Malian Sage Tierno Bokar Taal perceives faith to be in three stages: solid, liquid and gas. In the first, the people of this disposition cannot distinguish between the essence of faith and their understanding of it. In fact, they are willing to declare war against anyone who perceives faith differently than them.

In the second, the essence of faith is pure water, while its form is the color and shape of the container, as al-Junayd described *ma'rifa* (gnosis).

Meanwhile, the last state of gaseous faith is subtle air that rises to heaven, residing at the summit of mastery and perceiving all the paths towards the peak with ease.

Incidentally, Goethe described music as liquid architecture and architecture as frozen music. Artists in general can only be those with the disposition of liquid faith.

Art is essentially the process of perceiving a singular essence in different forms. For what is a story but weaving a narrative of *tawhīd* (oneness) across different settings and characters?

But among all the artforms, the musician is the one who truly perceives the rhythm of reality in its original form: as an incessant river of sound, a deluge gushing forth from the singular breath of *Kun*, which is naught but air.

99

In *Muhammad: The Messenger of Islam*, Hajjah Aminah 'Adil describes the primordial vision of the Prophet Muhammad's ﷺ light and form in the spiritual sphere prior to existence in this material realm.

Each of us perceived a different limb of the prophetic body, and depending on what we saw, it foretold our disposition and path in life as a craft towards the summit of mastery and *walāya* (sainthood).

Those who saw the palms of his sands ﷺ were destined to become calligraphers, while those who saw his eyebrows ﷺ became painters. Those who saw his feet ﷺ became judges. And those who saw his shadow ﷺ became musicians.

However, as the Prophet's companion Abu Bakr explains, during his migration with the Prophet ﷺ from Mecca to Medina, he noticed that the latter does not have a shadow. And so, what did musicians actually perceive in the primordial realm?

I contemplated this question for a long time and realized that musicians perceived a dimension of the Prophet ﷺ that nobody else could.

If, as Ibn al-'Arabi states, saints inherit the prophetic spiritual states and breaths, whereas scholars merely inherit his actions and statements ﷺ, then music is one of the purest paths to sainthood, for it only is the immediate child of breath.

It is not enough for a musician to listen and produce music. The challenge is living a musical life, a task much easier said than done. And this is not simply about having a perfect rhythm in our daily life or proverbially dancing the perfect melody with our surroundings.

Rather, the focus should be on constantly and incessantly translating from the world of music to music of the world. We present a broken series of meditations that stand as an attempt to highlight beauty despite our shortcomings.

Our music should be the golden glue that holds our brokenness together as is the case in the Japanese art of Kintsugi. Music is an act of repentance, *tawba*, which translates to 'returning to God'.

The canvas of our music is a safe space wherein we feel comfortable to confess our ugliness to the guide within our musical instrument, who then turns around and dresses these faults in a garment of concealment and beauty.

Music is a silent acknowledgment of everything that we are too shy to admit about ourselves, even to ourselves in complete silence, but can do so to our instruments in their absolute stillness.

We do this because we trust in the redemptive process that ensues. I present my vices in a story of *maqāmāt* and say: "My Lord, I am insincere in doing what you have asked. The best I can do is capture the beauty of sound without. So, please make me sound within!"

Conclusion

Where words fail, music speaks
– Hans Christian Andersen

This book has been a decades-long sojourn in the making. What I have shared with you in the previous pages has been my own journey, no one else's, despite the similarities that others might share with my perspectives. I also anticipate the disagreements others might have with my opinions.

Much like my previous book, *A Nostalgic Remembrance: Sufism and the Breath of Creativity*, this work is neither an academic monograph on the history of Arabic music nor music in Islam. Rather, it is a meditation on the sacred role of sound and music in the Middle East, taking into consideration both history and metaphysics.

Naturally, this also reflects my own taste in music as the author of this book. For instance, although I have mentioned John Coltrane and Yusuf Abd al-Latif, Jazz is not really the genre of my path as a musician. Rather, it is Arabic music and the art of *maqāmāt* that has been the canvas and palette of my meditations on the craft of music as a journey to God.

The three main chapters of the book: History, Metaphysics and Reflections – with a preamble on *maqāmāt* in between the second and third sections – are like disparate threads that overlap at various intersections and connect together as different settings for the same story. These approaches to music have also been my palette of methods through which I have come to negotiate the sacred role of sound and Islam in my life.

I understand that what I have set out to accomplish in this book might be precarious for many, simply because I am not yet an accomplished musician, so that beginning artists might gain something from a masterclass that I offer on music. On the contrary, I acknowledge that I am neither an accomplished nor well-known oudist.

However, what I do know is Islamic metaphysics, specifically Ibn al-'Arabi's teachings which is the focus of my doctoral dissertation and has been at the center of my life's work over the past decade. I also grew up in a family of – visual – artists. My migration and diaspora from my country of birth, Iraq, due to the First Gulf War, has given me a unique appreciation of the arts as a language for negotiating one's identity in a globalized world.

In addition to all of this, I have worked in the American Muslim community for over two decades as an educator, where I witnessed a drastically different approach to the arts than my childhood experience in Iraq, Egypt and Jordan. This has been one of the main motivational forces behind my nonprofit organization, the *Adhwaq Center for Spirituality, Culture and the Arts*, where I focus on 'spirituality and creativity in contemporary culture'.

I have been driven for the past few decades by another cultural possibility for Muslims in the West; a vision where Muslims are known not only for mosques and seminaries but also music and film schools. I am hopeful of a future where Islam is translated, not only linguistically from Arabic, Turkish and Farsi, but also culturally to the Western lens, through the highest metaphysical pinnacle of Islamic thought: Ibn al-'Arabi's works.

In order for this to be accomplished, I believe Islam can no longer remain a 'static system of rituals and beliefs', as modernity and the secularization project have set out to reduce and repackage all religions, and as many Muslims have unfortunately adopted as the traditional view of Islam. Rather, I hold that a dimension of Islam must emerge that fits Shahab Ahmed's description, as a 'process of making meaning'.

The litmus test here is simple: can Islam be interpreted, translated and presented in a way such that it can improve the lives of humanity without the need for conversion? The current paradigm and *da'wa* (calling to God) discourse by Muslims presents the modern world as an abomination that can only be fixed by Islam (i.e., if everybody becomes Muslim). But despite the fact that Islam remains one of the fastest growing religions in the world, the counter statistic is not considered: how many converts and native-born Muslims leave the faith altogether?

During the past two decades, I have heard of many young Muslims leaving their faith altogether or worse, committing suicide. Some of these kids were even enrolled in Islamic schools in the United States. The crisis is actually the same for both types of Muslim youth, those in Islamic and public schools: a lackluster religious education that fails to make Islam relevant in the modern world.

Over the past few decades, there have been countless Islamic seminaries springing all over the United States, many of which teach exactly the same texts (e.g., jurisprudence, theology, *hadith*, Quranic sciences and moral ethical Sufism). The craft of religious scholarship has been nominated by modern Muslims as the exclusive path to *walāya* (sainthood). This in itself is a modern invention, an attempt to imprison religion within its own sphere, away from everyday life.

Thus, carpentry, tailoring, music, poetry, acting and countless other crafts are no longer viable means for sainthood, whereas traditionally in the past these were the paths to God most suitable for the masses. Whereas scholasticism was an elitist enterprise and the masses enjoined memorization and recitation of Sufi poetry and music-making as the means for sacralizing their daily life, nowadays the formula is inverted: everybody wants to be a scholar but very few are interested in 'what makes us human'.

In *A Nostalgic Remembrance*, I discuss all of the above from the perspective the arts generally. In this book, I finally have the opportunity to delve into my passion, Arabic music. I tried to show how music, both historically and metaphysically, is a path to God in Islam. I hope both Muslim and non-Muslim readers discover a reality of this faith that rebuts much of the propaganda today.

Indeed, in the present day, Islam is not a faith that is associated with the arts or music. On the contrary, it is a religion that is tethered to violence, iconoclasm, rigidity and many other negative connotations. Unfortunately, Muslims are not entirely innocent when it comes to these depictions. Consider, for example, that a study among Islamic schools in the West revealed that the most common vocabulary term among students in these institutions is 'obligatory'.

How many mosques, Islamic schools or seminaries across the West teach the liberal arts? How many of them teach musical theory or practice? It was not that long ago, in the 18th century, that Muslim scholars taught these topics in Mecca and Medina as part of the religious curriculum. Today, the most common motif in these institutions is that music is *harām* (forbidden) or controversial. As the Islamic maxim states: "The one who does not have something cannot give it."

Even the controversy surrounding translations of Mawlana Rumi's poetry in the last few years, with headlines that read: "How the West took Islam out of Rumi" misses the point entirely, that Muslims had for centuries exiled Rumi, Ibn al-'Arabi and countless other Sufi saints out of Islam. Let us find a single Islamic school or seminary that teaches Rumi's *Mathnawi* in the West, much less Ibn al-'Arabi's *Bezels* or *Meccan Openings*.

And here is the central dilemma: If the Muslim community today refuses to teach its own heritage, including Rumi's and Ibn al-'Arabi's works at its institutions then how can they offer classes on Naguib Mahfouz, Khalil Gibran or any of the literary giants from the East? More importantly, how can they delve into Emerson, Frost or Shakespeare? And let us be frank: without teaching pillars of the liberal arts in the West, such as these figures mentioned here, there can never be a healthy cultural existence for Muslims in the world today.

And it is for this reason that I focused on the sacred role of sound and music in this book, alongside the fact that it is my passion. This is pertinent considering that music remains one of the most controversial issues for Western Muslims. I still get questions today about the evidence for the validity of singing and musical instruments, despite the fact that it is one of the most basic forms of creative expression in the universe. It is also particularly troublesome because music is a central medium for spiritual expression in the West, which has led me elsewhere to say that Islam cannot survive in the West if music is not embraced by Muslims.

Conclusion

The most important fact I tried to show in the preceding chapters is that Islam is, first and foremost, a sound-oriented and musical faith. Historically, Islam began with an utterance: *Iqra'!* (Recite) while metaphysically, all of creation began with the Divine Voice: *Kun!* Sound precedes form in the Quran, while God's Hearing heralds His Vision. The revelation of the Quran was always annunciated by sounds, either the humming of bees, ringing of bells or metal chains dragged across pebbles.

The Prophet Muhammad ﷺ tethered the meanings of the Quran to *nagham* (melodies) and emphasized its importance. There is no way around the centrality of sound and its sacredness in this early beginning of the faith. And then, we discover that later Muslim generations, immediately following the Prophet's passing, were musicians and singers, a tradition that continued until the 18th century and the advent of Wahhabism.

It is safe to say that the modern controversy surrounding music and musical instruments was never widespread among premodern Muslims. Rather, it was always a matter of scholarly debate, which neither dictated nor affected the daily lives of the masses. As Shahab Ahmed mentions, traditionally there were two sources of authority in Muslim communities, the 'prescriptive' censure of the scholars and 'explorative' prerogative of individual Muslims to 'make meaning' in their own lives.

One can say that this book explores this second source of authority, specifically pertaining to music as a sacred craft and path to God for

Muslim musicians. Ibn al-'Arabi shows us the extent to which producing and consuming music is rooted in the spiritual dimension of Islamic cosmology. The first instance of *tarab* (musical ecstasy), according to Ibn al-'Arabi, is experienced not by human beings, but the throne of God when it hears the descent of the Divine Creative Command *Kun*. All subsequent instances of *tarab* are mirror reflections of this original movement.

Ibn al-'Arabi tethers this spiritual *tarab* to musical instruments, whereby the sounds produced by the oud and other means are the result of the rotations of the heavenly orbits that also experience *tarab* and reflect that in a musician's hands. This allows the Andalusian mystic to discuss the different stages of *samā'* (listening) to melody and music.

He ultimately tethers the deluge of emotions one feels when listening to music or melody to *ma'rifa* (Divine Gnosis). Ibn al-'Arabi's vision is a unitive one. The *tarab* experienced by the Divine Throne is never divorced from the ecstasy felt by those listening to Mustafa Ismail, Umm Kulthum, Riyad al-Sunbati, John Coltrane or Adele. Rather, these are varying degrees of ecstasy, not experiences contradictory or exclusive to one another.

For me personally, the Golden Age of Arabic music is the zenith of the marriage between the two arts of Quran recitation and secular music, with an unbreakable bond held together by the ocean of *maqāmāt* (modalities of Arabic music). I approached this topic from countless conversations and hours of research motivated by my own passion for this artform and born from a childhood experience of being moved to tears by the *maqām* of a *mu'adhdhin* in Jordan, and many other similar experiences that I continue to have today.

Simply thinking about *maqāmāt* makes me happy. It is a safe space that I can retreat to when life becomes difficult. When I cannot figure out the melodic progression of my surroundings, I only need to play a *taqsīm* on the oud and envision a narrative of sound that makes musical sense and provides hope in the face of uncertainty.

Most importantly, this applies to me and countless other people because music and sound is how we process reality. This is an altogether different dimension to the importance of music and musicians in the Muslim community specifically and any society generally. Musicians are not only important because they produce songs that are nice to hear in one's free time. Rather, they are the means through which God communicates knowledge to a community through the medium of sound.

And as I outline in *A Nostalgic Remembrance*, each of the art mediums (written, visual, auditory and moving) represent a stage in the creative as well as human process. The written arts teach us about grammar, eloquence and drafts, all of which manifest to varying degrees in other art forms. We can also speak about the grammar of medicine, eloquence of engineering, poetry of computer science and the draft of building a car.

The visual arts instruct us to pay attention to the texture of a medium and how that might be used to convey meaning. Also, how does architecture, sculpture and painting each engage with the audience differently? As for the auditory arts, I focus on the importance of silence and listening as a carrier of meaning. In this book, however, I am much more interested in how music and sound help us become musical beings.

All of the elements of music (e.g., notes, melody, rhythm, tempo, ornamentation) translate to human behaviors. Given the centrality of sound in Islam, historically and metaphysically, we can comfortably say that a good human being, Islamically, is one who is a sound symphony. This is the highest objective, accomplished by cultivating the arts generally and music specifically. Inversely, what is lost by neglecting creativity and musical education is, first, the loss of music and musicians and, conclusively, forgetting the inability to live a musical life.

Where we find ourselves today is that many Quran reciters have beautiful voices but without a clue as to how to use melody to augment the meanings of the Quran and move the listener emotionally. We also find the proliferation of religious singers who appropriate melodies composed by giants like al-Mouji, Baleegh and others without giving credit where it is due. Why are they borrowing these melodies to begin with? Because, simply, they cannot compose their own.

As a Muslim musician who is also deeply immersed in the culture of Arabic music, I can confidently say that today Muslims are not major contributors to this craft. Rather, we find mostly Christian Arabs like Simon Shaheen and others who are its custodians, weaving the siren song at the summit. Even among many of the Muslim Arab musicians, very few – if any – are excavating the subtleties of music from Islamic metaphysics, as Ibn al-'Arabi, al-Farabi or al-Kindi did.

I wrote this book as an Arab and Muslim musician who is hopeful of a future when we musicians and artists can be seen as creative custodians of our faiths. I am eager for a moment in time when we no longer need validation for listening or producing music and can grow, as a community, in being musical beings. This is already where I linger as a musician, but I do not wish to be a solitary note in this *maqām*.

Postscript by Pot Amir

Nusantara's greatest artist, P.Ramlee met his future second wife Norizan, when she was still married to the Ruler of Perak Sultan Yusuf Izuddin Shah when the Sultan hosted a number of Malaya's movie stars at a Grand Dinner Show in Ipoh in the 50's.

Before introducing P.Ramlee to Norizan, the Sultan had actually warned her of the magnetic powers of P.Ramlee's eyes and specifically told her to not ever look directly in the young actor's eyes. Of course, that was the thing that she did, and the rest is history.

My Teacher, my Guide, the writer of this magnificent book told me "to not overthink", so…

We the artists are the most misunderstood lot. Heck, we don't even understand ourselves most of the time. But a Muslim artist climbs higher, more treacherous mountains no doubt. Double that if you are a *Muslimat*.

There are 3 paradigm-shifting moments in my path as an artist.

1. First time I ever met Habib Umar Bin Hafidh and listening to a rendition of his famous Mawlid.
   - Led me to the decision to abandon all my other modes of singing to join the Selawat Ensemble known as 'Al Mawlid'
2. First time I ever held a 'keris' (a traditional Malay sword, with symbolism much like that of what a 'jambiya' is to a Yemeni) was the day I met a Malay Habib, who upon putting the keris in my hand, told me to "not vacate my seat", for somebody more destructive to the ummah might occupy it. Loud and clear. I had to go back in.
3. First time I had to write a postscript (okay, I had to google "postscript") was for this book; is also the first time I managed to finish reading a fairly academic book without dozing off or abandoning it altogether, like all the other fallen comrades before it. In the course of reading it, I found myself exclaiming countless times "Yes!!! That's what I'm talking about!!!" and even "I knew it!!!" Things I couldn't really word in an eloquent manner are spelt out in the open right in most of the pages. Alhamdulillah.

And very much like The Writer, I vehemently agree, as musicians or artists, we have lingered long enough. Mostly to try to explain "our art" but worst still, getting caught in the lure of the LCD displays of our gadgets for the love of art (yeah, sure).

We have seen legendary Muslim artists and saints alike, leaving us too soon, to which we always say, "Allah loves them more". *Allah Yarham* (God have Mercy) on Sudirman Hj Arshad who left us at a mere age of 38, while the eternal Nusantara Legend P.Ramlee, or *Allah Yarham* Teuku Zakaria bin Teuku Nyak Putih who passed at only 45.

So, if you happen to be an Artist, who is a "not-bad" Muslim who loves art so much you can't explain why, the "*maqam*" (being the last word of this book) is to recalibrate our intentions, at least firstly, I think. Remember again that Allah loves us more than a mother does a child.

And if we believe that we are destined for greatness or so we strive, like the gone-too-soon legends before us, we ought to assume that we'd be gone anytime soon. One year before his death, P.Ramlee had known all that is to know about the music business and film industry after years of toiling and trials-and-errors. He had a whole consortium of people and funders willing to jump along with him.

Heck, he even enrolled in a 3-month Japanese Language course at the Japanese Embassy of Kuala Lumpur. Had he been alive, KL could have been an international hub for independent arts. But as the legend goes, Allah loves him more. I don't want to ever see him in his 90's trying out a TikTok trend either. *Al Fatihah*

Going back to the *maqam*, I don't know about all y'all, but after just one reading of this milestone of a book, this unschooled artist is now firm, my *maqam* says I ought to hurry and start aligning myself with "smiling-kinda people" (RE: Suruhanjaya Senyum) and assembling my panel of reliable 3Fs:- Family, Friends and Funders who understand, my "Final Network" if you must, #finaleleven.

No time to linger. No Man is an Island. Just that my small island MUST consists of Smiley people, and if they are Muslims, they MUST be amongst those who love all the Mawlids, *Tahlils*, The Saints and the whole package.

I ain't got no time to be debating fools bebeh, I'm going to die as a legend you don't never forget. Besides, if I have Selawat Lovers with me, I also have in my team of #finaleleven Allah, the angels and the strongest of Believers.

Every Single Friday. We are reminded. Yet we forget.

> *"Verily, Allah and (all) His angels send blessings and greetings on the Holy Prophet (blessings and peace be upon him). O believers! Invoke blessings on him and salute him with a worthy salutation of peace abundantly (and fervently)."*
> (Al-Ahzab :56)

Postscript

www.ingramcontent.com/pod-product-compliance
Lightning Source LLC
Chambersburg PA
CBHW030548080526
44585CB00012B/300